AMERICAN DREAM
NO ONE'S COMING TO SAVE YOU: PREPARE TO SUCCEED IN AN AI WORLD
BRADLEY R AMAN

Table of Contents

Foreword

Over the last three years, I've spent time in cities big and small across this country. I've walked through airports, stayed in hotels, sat in business offices, spoken with tradesmen, met college students, shared coffee with plant managers, and listened closely to the quiet conversations happening beneath the noise of everyday life.

At first, most people didn't seem concerned.

Artificial intelligence felt like something happening somewhere else. A Silicon Valley story. A tech headline. Something for coders, billionaires, and conference stages.

The average American worker still believed what generations before them had been taught to believe: work hard, stay loyal, build experience, and your future will take care of itself.

For a while, the country still looked normal.

The hotel front desk was staffed.

The call center was full.

The junior analyst was still building spreadsheets.

The college student still believed the degree automatically led to opportunity.

The office lights were still on.

But underneath that normal surface, something had already started to shift.

I began noticing it in the conversations people were having behind closed doors. Executives weren't talking about expansion the way they had just a few years earlier. They were talking about software deployments, task automation, AI copilots, customer service compression, and how many roles could be reduced without public attention.

I'm not writing this as a career counselor, financial advisor, or motivational speaker repeating old rules that no longer work.

I'm writing this as someone who has spent a lifetime building businesses, hiring people, watching industries shift, and reinventing alongside the economy itself.

I learned sales and margins at ten years old, selling packs of gum door to door in my neighborhood. Later, I climbed the corporate ladder, learning firsthand how relationships, trust, and performance open doors that résumés alone never will.

At thirty-five, I stepped into entrepreneurship, building an online commercial kitchen supply business when e-commerce was still unfamiliar territory to most people. From there, I built a service company from one van and one customer into the largest operation of its kind in the United States before successfully exiting the business.

I have spent decades watching markets evolve, customer behavior shift, technology reshape industries, and entire business models rise and disappear.

I know what disruption looks like before it makes headlines because I've had to move with it my entire career.

That is why I can tell you with absolute certainty: what is happening right now is different.

At first, even the technology leaders spoke with swagger.

They stood on stages and talked about innovation, efficiency, and the future with the kind of confidence that makes everyone in the room assume they had full control over what was coming.

Then something changed.

I watched that swagger turn into urgency.

Then urgency became a sprint.

The same people who had once stepped confidently toward the AI era were now running toward it at full speed, not because they had solved the consequences, but because they knew how quickly it would begin absorbing tasks, then jobs, then departments, and eventually entire occupations.

And while they sprinted, most American workers kept standing still.

That is the danger.

The greatest risk in this new era is not that AI is coming.

It's that millions of people are still pretending it isn't already here.

I've sat across from workers in industries that once looked untouchable.

A hotel front desk clerk quietly wonders how long it would be before self-service kiosks and AI booking systems reduce the overnight staff.

A powerline worker is asking whether grid automation and predictive systems will eventually shrink the number of field crews needed in his region.

An aircraft salesman is wondering if AI-driven procurement tools and virtual sales ecosystems will make relationship-based selling less valuable.

A nurse's assistant asking whether clinical AI, workflow automation, and remote diagnostics will reduce the roles people once assumed required a permanent human presence.

These are not lazy people.

These are people who were unlucky.

These are hard-working Americans who did exactly what they were told to do.

Get the degree.

Take the job.

Stay loyal.

Build the résumé.

Trust the company.

Trust the system.

Trust the future.

But the system they trusted is changing faster than most institutions are willing to admit.

Schools still prepare students for entry-level jobs that are disappearing.

Companies still talk about loyalty while reducing headcount through quiet software rollouts.

Families still assume stability works the way it did twenty years ago.

It doesn't.

The old contract is breaking.

For generations, Americans believed that hard work alone would protect them. That if you showed up, stayed consistent, and proved yourself, the ladder would still be there to climb.

That ladder is being rebuilt in real time.

Some rungs are disappearing.

Others are moving.

And entirely new ladders are being built for the people willing to adapt faster than everyone else.

This book was not written to spread fear.

Fear without a roadmap is useless.

This book was written because I believe the American Dream is still alive, but it now belongs to the people who prepare early, move decisively, and refuse to bury their heads in the sand while the world changes around them.

That responsibility now belongs to every one of us.

It belongs to the college student choosing a major.

The middle manager is protecting a family.

The tradesman is thinking about ownership.

The entrepreneur is looking for the next shift.

The parent teaches their children how the world really works.

The American Dream was never meant to be inherited passively.

It must be protected actively.

As a veteran, I feel a deep obligation to remind every American of something bigger than career strategy or financial survival.

Achieving the American Dream is your call to duty.

You may not have served in the Armed Forces, but in this new era, you are now the commander of your own mission: protecting your future, your family, your income, and the opportunities that make this country exceptional.

The battlefield may look different today.

It may be a classroom, a job site, a small business, a boardroom, a trade school, a hospital floor, or a late night at the kitchen table learning the tools that will define the next economy.

But the principle remains the same.

You fight hard for the continued greatness of this country by refusing complacency, by adapting faster than the forces trying to make you irrelevant, and by building a life strong enough to carry the next generation forward.

The American Dream survives only when its people are willing to defend it through discipline, courage, ownership, and relentless action.

In this era, no one can take command of that mission for you.

That responsibility is now yours.

This AI era will not reward the most comfortable.

It will reward the most aware.

The most adaptable.

The most relentless.

The families who talk about change early.

The workers who learn before they are forced to.

The leaders who decide to own the future instead of being managed by it.

That is why this book exists.

Not to scare you.

To prepare you.

Because the truth is simple, brutal, and freeing:

No one is coming to save you.

Which means your future is still yours to build.

Chapter 1

The Day Stability Broke

When the Dam Breaks

For years, stability in America felt like a dam standing tall above the valley.

Massive.

Concrete.

Permanent.

People built their entire lives downstream from it.

Mortgages.

College plans.

Retirement accounts.

Family routines.

Vacation traditions.

A child's first car.

The belief that next year will be better than this year.

The dam was the old promise:

work hard, stay loyal, and the structure holding your future in place would remain strong.

At first, the cracks were too small to notice.

A department quietly downsized.

An internship program disappeared.

A front desk replaced by kiosks.

A call center floor cut in half.

A young graduate is sending out hundreds of résumés and hearing nothing back.

Tiny fractures.

Hairline pressure points.

Easy to dismiss if you only looked at the surface.

That is how dam failures begin.

Not with instant collapse.

With silent pressure building behind walls, people still trust.

Technology accelerated.

Labor costs rose.

Software improved.

Executive incentives changed.

Shareholder pressure intensified.

AI began absorbing tasks that once justified entire careers.

The water kept rising.

Most people never saw the danger because, from the outside, the structure still looked intact.

The paycheck still arrived.

The title was still on the business card.

The office still had lights on.

The degree still hung on the wall.

The dam still looked strong.

But when the pressure finally reaches critical mass, the break does not happen politely.

It happens all at once.

The wall gives way.

What once felt permanent becomes an unstoppable force.

The flood that follows is layoffs, hiring freezes, wage compression, vanished entry-level roles, shrinking middle management, and entire occupations being rerouted into smaller teams powered by software.

The families downstream do not have time to debate whether the water is real.

They move, or they get overtaken.

That is where millions of workers are now.

The day stability broke was not the day people first noticed AI.

It was the day the invisible pressure behind the old system finally became too great for the old promises to hold.

And once a dam breaks, pretending the wall is still standing is the fastest way to drown.

More Stories Like This Everywhere

In early 2026, John walked into work expecting an ordinary Friday.

For fifteen years, he had worked as a data analyst for a national insurance company. He was reliable, respected, and known for finding ways to help the company process customer payments faster and more efficiently. He wasn't flashy, but he was dependable. The kind of employee companies used to build careers around.

John had done everything right.

He worked hard. He stayed loyal. He adapted to new software systems. He trained younger employees.

At home, his life looked solid. Four young kids. A stay-at-home wife. Mortgage payments. School activities. The normal chaos of a growing family was built around the belief that steady work meant steady security.

That morning, HR called.

He assumed it was about a system change or maybe a departmental update.

Instead, he was told his position had been eliminated.

The company had deployed a new AI-driven system that automated much of the analysis and forecasting that his team once handled. The software could process data faster, cheaper, and around the clock. Leadership framed it as modernization.

His role, and several others, simply weren't needed anymore.

He was offered a severance package and escorted out.

Fifteen years of loyalty ended in a fifteen-minute meeting.

At first, John believed he would quickly find another position. After all, he had experience, strong performance reviews, and a solid résumé.

But the job market had changed.

Many companies were deploying similar systems. Openings were limited. Positions that did exist often paid less or required different skills. Months passed. Savings dwindled. Stress mounted.

Eventually, the family burned through what they had set aside for emergencies and college funds. Pride gave way to necessity.

John went back to school.

He enrolled in a trade program and began training in electrical load forecasting and grid systems management, a field where skilled technicians now use AI tools to manage energy demand and infrastructure systems.

It wasn't the career he had imagined for himself fifteen years earlier. But it was work that still needed humans, people who understood systems, who could troubleshoot problems in the real world when technology alone couldn't solve them.

The transition was humbling. Financially painful. Emotionally exhausting.

But it worked.

Today, John is employed again. The path was harder than he expected, and the lesson came at a cost he never anticipated.

His mistake wasn't incompetence.

His mistake was believing stability still worked the way it did when he started his career.

His story is becoming common.

This book is not about some distant future where machines someday replace workers. It is about what is happening right now, shifts in hiring, job security, trust, wages, and upward mobility that are already reshaping careers across America.

Entry-level jobs are disappearing. Entire departments are being reduced after quiet software deployments. Hiring systems are overwhelmed by fake candidates. Digital impersonation is becoming routine. Workers are being monitored, measured, and replaced faster than they can adapt.

And most people do not see it coming until it hits them personally.

For generations, Americans were told that if they worked hard, stayed loyal, and followed the rules, stability would follow. Companies rewarded commitment. Industries supported lifelong careers. Experience protected you.

That contract is breaking.

Not because workers failed, but because technology, economics, and corporate incentives now move faster than institutions meant to protect them.

Governments move slowly. Corporations move in their own interests. Technology moves at full speed.

That leaves one person responsible for your future.

You.

This book is not written to scare you. It is written to prepare you.

Because the worst outcomes are not inevitable, but they are predictable if people remain unprepared.

The workers and families who succeed in the next decade will not simply be the smartest or luckiest. They will be the ones who recognize change early and adapt before disruption forces them to.

The American Dream is still alive.

But the safety nets people once trusted are not.

And whether you are twenty-two or fifty-two, the reality is the same:

No one is coming to save you.

The good news is you no longer need permission to save yourself.

Chapter 2

The New Illusion

After World War II, the United States entered one of the greatest periods of economic expansion in modern history.

Factories that once produced bombers, engines, steel plating, field radios, and military vehicles shifted into consumer goods, housing materials, automobiles, appliances, and the industrial equipment that would build modern America. Highways stretched across the country. Suburbs emerged almost overnight. Manufacturing boomed. Corporate America matured.

But the real story was not just industrial expansion. It was the transfer of skill.

Millions of returning soldiers were not coming home empty-handed. They brought back capabilities forged under pressure. Some had learned mechanics working on trucks, tanks, and aircraft engines. Some had developed management discipline leading men, logistics chains, supply depots, and field operations. Others came home with training in communications, navigation, aerodynamics, electrical systems, medicine, welding, fabrication, and heavy equipment maintenance.

The war had forced rapid technical education at scale. Young men who might never have touched advanced machinery in civilian life suddenly understood engines, hydraulics, structural systems, emergency medicine, scheduling, chain of command, and mission execution.

Those skills did not disappear when the uniforms came off. They became the backbone of the American middle class.

Aircraft mechanics moved into commercial aviation and aerospace. Motor pool specialists became fleet managers, diesel mechanics, and industrial repair experts. Combat medics became nurses, technicians, and healthcare administrators. Radio and radar operators transitioned into telecommunications and early electronics. Engineering corps veterans helped shape infrastructure, bridges, utilities, and large-scale construction. Quartermasters and officers moved naturally into plant supervision, operations leadership, transportation, warehousing, and executive management.

This is the honest part modern readers often miss. The post-war boom was not just luck. It was an intentional conversion of military skill into civilian productivity.

Government policy supported that conversion because leaders understood something fundamental: A stable, skilled working population creates a stable nation.

The GI Bill expanded access to universities, trade schools, and technical programs. VA-backed mortgages opened the door to home ownership. Federal highway projects fueled demand for construction labor, engineering, trucking, and industrial materials. Massive investments in manufacturing, aviation, medicine, and infrastructure gave returning workers places to apply what they had learned.

This was good for families. It was good for local communities. And it was good for the country.

Skilled workers earned reliable wages. Those wages bought homes, cars, insurance, appliances, and education for the next generation. That spending supported small businesses, local banks, schools, and municipal services. A stronger tax base funded roads, public safety, education, and future expansion.

The system worked because skill, policy, industry, and national interest were aligned.

A welder became a homeowner. A mechanic became a plant supervisor. A medic built a healthcare career. An officer became an executive. A generation that had endured chaos helped build order.

Before my father, **Raymond Aman**, ever returned home in 1947, his story had already been shaped by a kind of hardship that modern readers can barely imagine.

He was a boy in the Midwest when the Great Depression hit. His family lived in a sod shanty by the river, a place without heat, without comfort, and without the simple dignity of running water. He did not see indoor plumbing until high school.

His father, my grandfather, was unemployed for stretches of that brutal era, laying brick streets for the entity, "Civilian Conservation Corps", & "New Deal work relief program" just to earn enough food support to keep the family alive.

Then came the kind of loss that either breaks a child forever or hardens him into something unshakable.

His mother, pushed beyond her breaking point by the relentless pressure of poverty, took her own life when Raymond was just nine years old.

Most people would have been crushed under the weight of that beginning. But not my father.

At sixteen, he lied about his age and joined the United States Army Air Corps, "World War II military aviation branch". Before most boys had learned to shave, he was flying combat missions in a B-17 Flying Fortress," World War II heavy bomber", serving as a top-turret gunner and risking his life every time the aircraft crossed hostile skies.

He learned courage in the sky. He learned resilience under fire. He learned that preparation, precision, and trust in the men around you meant survival.

The war did more than give him technical training. It transformed a boy pulled from absolute poverty into a man prepared to manage people, grow operations, and build something larger than himself.

It gave him discipline. Systems thinking. Accountability. Calm under pressure. Leadership. The ability to make decisions when consequences were real.

That strength is what he eventually carried home. And that strength is what he passed on to me.

In 1947, my father, **Raymond Aman**, returned home carrying far more than a duffel bag and a discharge paper. He brought back discipline, technical precision, leadership habits, and the kind of calm decision-making that military training hardwires into a man.

His Army Air Corps training had taught him how to think in systems. Process mattered. Timing mattered. Accountability mattered. Small mistakes compounded. Preparation prevented failure.

Those lessons transferred naturally into civilian life. When he came home, he went to work for **Safeway Food Stores**, starting as an assistant manager. At first glance, retail might seem worlds away from military aviation support, but the greater skills were identical. Inventory discipline. People management. Operational systems. Logistics. Chain-of-command decision-making. Performance standards.

What the military had taught him about keeping systems running under pressure now translated into keeping stores efficient, teams accountable, and customers served.

Over the next forty years, my father built a career that the old American system was designed to reward. He moved up steadily. The assistant manager became the store's leader. Store leadership became a broader operational responsibility. Eventually, through discipline, reliability, and the ability to lead people and processes, he rose to **district manager**.

That mattered for more than professional pride. It built a family. It created stability. It turned military discipline into middle-class security. A long career produced predictable income, community standing, home ownership, and the kind of tax-paying, community-supporting household that strengthened the country around him.

This is the honest truth about that generation. The system worked because men like my father converted military structure into civilian productivity, and the nation had institutions ready to reward it. Government support, private industry expansion, trade discipline, and managerial ladders all pointed in the same direction.

So my father built the kind of life millions of Americans were taught to admire. He built security. And security worked.

But beneath that success, something subtle was happening.

In exchange for stability, workers slowly surrendered control.

We traded ownership for employment. We traded autonomy for payroll. We traded leverage for routine. We traded optionality for benefits.

The prison was never visible because it was comfortable.

The bars were not steel. They were health insurance tied to an employer. Retirement is tied to tenure. Promotion tied to internal approval. Income tied to someone else's balance sheet.

Generations were conditioned to believe security flowed downward from institutions instead of upward from personal ownership, adaptability, and leverage.

It worked because industrial growth required manpower. Scaling meant hiring. Expansion meant headcount. Loyalty and obedience were rewarded because labor was essential to growth.

But dependency only feels safe while the structure itself remains stable. And structures always shift.

That shift is where today's workers find themselves.

In 1955, growth meant more workers, more supervisors, and more offices. Growth was physical. It was visible. It expanded the middle class because companies needed people to scale.

In 2026, growth often means the opposite.

Automation. Optimization. AI-assisted systems. Cloud-based workflows. Software that multiplies output without multiplying payroll.

Industrial growth expanded opportunities through employment. AI-driven growth increasingly concentrates opportunity through leverage.

That is not cruelty. It is an incentive. Institutions optimize for efficiency. Technology accelerates that optimization. And loyalty compounds far slower than software upgrades.

This is the part many workers misread.

The environment changed. The rules that once built middle-class stability no longer create the same protection. The habits that once made careers safer can now make workers more exposed.

The old advice was not wrong. It was context-dependent. And the context has changed.

This chapter is not an attack on the past. The post-war system created extraordinary upward mobility for millions of families. It gave Americans dignity, home ownership, a predictable retirement, and a belief that work could create a better future.

But the same environment also trained people to confuse employment with control.

That confusion is dangerous in an AI-driven economy.

Today, the tools of leverage are available to individuals, small businesses, skilled trades, entrepreneurs, and fast-learning professionals in ways previous generations never had access to. The workers who adapt early, build systems, learn the tools, and move closer to judgment and ownership will widen their opportunity.

The ones who continue to rely exclusively on institutional insulation may discover too late that the insulation has thinned.

The lesson is not panic. It is clarity.

The old system rewarded compliance. The new system rewards leverage.

That is the stability illusion. And seeing it clearly is the first step toward building something stronger than the system that once protected you.

Chapter 3

The Lies We Inherited

Imagine my father, **Raymond Aman**, coming home not in 1947, but in the spring of 1991, after the historical event, the Gulf War & Operation Desert Storm.

The values would have been the same. Discipline. Duty. Reliability. The instinct to work harder than the next man. The willingness to start at the bottom and earn trust.

He still would have brought home the systems thinking the military taught him. Army Air Corps mechanics in World War II became Air Force logistics, aircraft systems, operations discipline, and command structure in the Desert Storm era. The bones of the man would not have changed.

He still would have gone to work for Safeway Grocery Stores. He still might have started as an assistant manager, learning store operations, inventory flow, people management, shrink control, scheduling, routing, and district-level logistics. He still would have risen through performance. Store manager. Regional leadership. Eventually, the district manager.

For a while, the story would have looked almost identical. A home. A family. A respectable income. A growing tax base. A belief that loyalty and competence create long-term stability.

But this is where the world changes.

By the 2000s, software began absorbing pieces of what once made a district manager valuable. Inventory forecasting becomes algorithmic. Store labor scheduling becomes automated. Supply-chain routing is optimized by enterprise systems. Sales trend analysis becomes dashboard-driven. Bookkeeping exceptions are flagged automatically. Customer service escalations are centralized. Regional reporting that once took managers days now happens in minutes.

At first, this feels like progress to my father, and he becomes more productive. He can oversee more stores. Make decisions faster. Move data instead of waiting for it.

But by 2015, the quiet shift becomes visible. The company no longer needs as many layers between store operations and executive leadership. The dashboards have replaced the meetings. The forecasts replaced the intuition. The scheduling systems replaced local judgment. The optimization software replaced much of the middle.

His title might still exist. But the economic value of the role has been thinned.

One Tuesday morning, after decades of loyalty, he is called into a conference room. Not because he failed. Because the workflow changed, AI-driven operational systems can now manage labor allocation, district reporting, inventory turns, vendor coordination, and performance benchmarking across hundreds of stores with fewer human decision points.

He walks out with a severance packet instead of a pension ceremony.

That is the difference between inherited values and expired context. The same man. The same discipline. The same willingness to build. A completely different structural ending.

This is not a criticism of previous generations. It is the clearest possible illustration of what changed.

The formula did not fail because my dad changed. It failed because the environment evolved past the assumptions that once protected men like him.

Every generation passes down the advice that helped it survive. That advice is rarely dishonest. More often, it is simply built for a world that no longer exists.

That is the tension at the center of this chapter. The enemy is not bad advice. It is an **expired context**.

The lessons previous generations handed down were earned through real struggle. Study hard. Get the degree. Work longer than everyone else. Stay loyal. Keep your head down. Climb patiently.

For decades, those principles worked because the labor market rewarded consistency, patience, and long skill cycles. Entry-level roles were real training grounds. Companies built ladders. Supervisors developed talent. Middle management expanded. Skills lasted long enough to build entire careers.

But the environment changed. Not all at once. Quietly. Then suddenly.

The inherited formula did not fail because people became lazy. It failed because the speed of technological change began to outpace the speed of institutional adaptation.

Part of that inherited formula began much earlier than most people realize. It began in the classroom.

The school systems that shaped workers in the 1940s and 1950s were built for the economy America was trying to scale. The country needed factory workers, retail clerks, bookkeepers, office support staff, salesmen to move the flood of new consumer products, supervisors, and dependable middle managers. The educational model reflected that reality.

Students were rewarded for punctuality. Following directions. Repeating process. Respecting hierarchy. Trusting management. Staying in line. Specializing in clearly defined roles.

That structure was not accidental. It matched the industrial machine that was building the American middle class. Factories needed consistency. Retail chains needed process discipline. Corporate systems needed clerical reliability. Mass expansion required people who could execute within proven systems.

That model helped produce one of the strongest tax bases in American history. Steady jobs led to predictable wages. Predictable wages created homeowners, consumers, savers, and taxpayers. The worker, the school, the corporation, and the government were all pointed in the same direction.

By the late 1980s and 1990s, that educational posture began to shift. Computer labs entered schools. Engineering pathways expanded. Business systems classes emerged. Students were pushed toward technology, software, analytical thinking, and more open-ended problem-solving. The digital economy needed more than obedience. It needed systems thinkers.

This generation learned to think more creatively and more freely. They were taught to solve problems, not just repeat tasks. Computer engineering, coding logic, data systems, design, business modeling, and project-based collaboration became increasingly valuable. That educational evolution helped produce the early digital workforce: analysts, programmers, engineers, technology consultants, financial modelers, and creative operators.

This changed the American worker. The identity shifted from industrial obedience to digital creativity. Workers no longer simply followed the process. They increasingly built, interpreted, modeled, and optimized systems.

But here is the hard truth that connects directly to this book. Schools almost always train workers for the economy institutions expect, not the ones arriving next.

That means every generation inherits a version of the labor market that is already beginning to expire. The industrial student was prepared for factories. The digital student was prepared for software. Now the AI era demands something different again: adaptability, judgment, workflow orchestration, and continuous reinvention.

The American worker has now lived through three different labor identities. Industrial obedience. Digital creativity. AI-era adaptability.

The pain many workers feel today is not because they failed. It is because the institutions that trained them were preparing them for the last cycle, while the market was already moving into the next one.

So let's name the inherited lies clearly.

Lie #1: Hard work alone guarantees upward mobility. Hard work still matters. It always will. But effort without leverage is now exposed. When AI can summarize, draft, route, forecast, schedule, reconcile, and communicate faster than a human working manually, effort alone no longer guarantees progress. The market increasingly rewards *amplified output*, not just long hours.

Lie #2: A degree secures stability. Education still matters. But credentials without adaptable skill stacks are no longer anchors. A degree that feeds directly into shrinking routine work can create fragility instead of security. Today, the more important question is not "what did you study?" but "what can you do that compounds with technology?"

Lie #3: Loyalty creates protection. This may be the most emotionally painful lie. Many workers were raised on the belief that if they gave a company decades of commitment, the company would protect them in return. That was often true in slower industrial cycles. It is far less reliable in quarterly optimization cycles driven by software adoption and margin pressure. Corporations reward value creation. They are rarely designed to preserve roles for sentimental reasons.

Lie #4: Experience automatically increases value. Experience still matters, but only when it evolves. Routine mastery in a shrinking workflow can become expensive history. The worker who keeps learning compounds value. The worker who assumes past competence automatically protects future relevance drifts toward compression.

Lie #5: Change moves slowly enough for you to keep up. This may be the most dangerous assumption of all. The AI era compresses what once took years into months. Workflow shifts happen before job titles change. Expectations rise before compensation does. Hiring standards move before schools update curriculum. Waiting for "clarity" often means waiting until the advantage is gone.

This shift is already visible in the very roles that previous generations assumed were safe stepping stones.

Customer service. Administrative support. Logistics coordination. Junior analysts. Entry-level coding. Bookkeeping. Dispatching. Claims processing. Basic compliance review.

These roles once served as the first rung of the ladder. They taught systems. Built judgment. Created supervisory pathways. Fed the middle class.

Now, many of them are becoming automation layers. AI handles ticket routing, report drafting, reconciliation, meeting notes, scheduling, support responses, first-pass coding, bookkeeping flags, and route optimization. The work often still exists. But fewer people are needed to do it.

That is why shrinking entry-level pathways matters so much. When the first rung thins, the entire ladder changes. The danger is not just fewer jobs today. There are fewer training paths to higher-income work tomorrow.

This is where readers need honesty without disrespect. Your parents were not wrong. Your teachers were not wrong. Your mentors were not wrong. They gave advice based on the labor market they inherited.

But inherited wisdom can become inherited fragility when the environment changes.

The right response is not resentment. It is recalibration.

You do not abandon hard work. You pair it with leverage. You do not reject education. You pair it with adaptability. You do not reject loyalty. You pair it with optionality. You do not reject experience. You force it to evolve.

That is the modern translation of the old virtues. The values still matter. The mechanics changed.

The families that adapt fastest in the next decade will not be the ones who panic. They will be the ones who update inherited wisdom before the market updates it for them.

More importantly, they will not fall to artificial intelligence. They will learn to use it.

The next American Dream will belong to families who treat AI as leverage instead of a threat. Parents who learn the tools early will protect their income longer. Workers who integrate AI into their workflows will widen their value instead of watching it narrow. Students taught adaptability, judgment, and systems thinking will enter stronger pathways than those trained for autopilot.

The winning families of the next decade will teach a new inheritance. Not blind loyalty to old ladders. But continuous learning. Optionality. Ownership. Creative problem solving. And the discipline to work *with* technology rather than pretend it is not reshaping the rules.

They will use AI to strengthen income. Protect dignity. Create resilience. And widen the American Dream for the next generation.

The lie was never in the values. The lie was believing the environment would stay the same.

The future still rewards discipline, work ethic, and responsibility. It simply now rewards the families who pair those virtues with adaptability faster than everyone around them.

Chapter 4

The Quiet Layoff

Most people imagine job loss as a single event.

A meeting.

A severance packet.

A badge that no longer works.

A drive home in silence.

But in the AI era, most layoffs begin long before anyone is formally let go.

They begin quietly.

Consider a young professional who did everything right.

He went to school to learn a specific task-based profession, the kind of work counselors, professors, and recruiters all said had a bright future. He studied hard, learned the systems, mastered the workflow, and graduated near the top of his class.

He landed a role at a top company. The kind of company people brag about getting into. The kind families celebrate at the dinner table because it feels like proof that the American Dream is still working.

From the beginning, he excelled.

His performance reviews were outstanding. His managers praised his consistency. He hit every metric. He solved problems quickly. He became the person others went to when something had to be done right.

Every signal around him reinforced the same belief: keep performing, and bigger opportunities will come.

A promotion.

More responsibility.

Leadership track.

A bigger office.

A stronger salary.

A stable future.

And for years, that belief felt justified.

Then the work began to change.

Not dramatically.

Quietly.

The reports he used to build from scratch started arriving pre-generated. Customer escalations were increasingly resolved before reaching his desk. Bookkeeping exceptions were flagged by the software. Route adjustments were optimized by AI. First-pass coding tasks were drafted automatically. The dashboards became smarter. The systems became faster.

At first, he felt more productive.

He interpreted this as growth.

He assumed the easier mechanics meant he was being freed for bigger strategic opportunities.

But the opportunity never widened.

Only the task list was narrowed.

The company still praised him. Still called him high potential. Still gave him strong reviews.

But fewer decisions required his judgment. Less of his day sharpened his skill. Less of the work prepared him for the next rung.

The title remained.

The future quietly disappeared.

That is the quiet layoff.

It begins when the work stops developing you, even while the paycheck continues.

The danger is that strong performers are often the last to suspect risk.

Praise creates psychological insulation.

Top reviews create the illusion that loyalty and excellence still guarantee a widening path.

But AI compression does not care how good you were at the old workflow.

It changes the workflow itself.

Then comes the Friday afternoon meeting.

HR asks if he has a few minutes.

He assumes it is about an organizational update, a restructuring discussion, maybe even a promotion conversation. After all, nothing in his recent feedback suggested danger.

Instead, he is told the company is realigning around new AI-enabled operational systems. His role has been eliminated. Certain responsibilities are being consolidated. Others are now fully automated.

The company appreciates his years of high performance.

A severance package is provided.

He walks out stunned.

Not because he failed.

Because every signal told him he was winning.

This is what makes the quiet layoff so psychologically devastating.

The worker is not blindsided by poor performance.

He is blindsided by **the disappearance of the pathway itself**.

The layoff did not begin that Friday.

It began months earlier when the work stopped building leverage.

When the learning curve flattened.

When the systems quietly absorbed the very tasks that once made the role valuable.

Before workers ever escape this pattern, most pass through a far more dangerous stage: denial.

The Head-in-the-Sand Stage

Americans do not usually lose jobs because they never saw change.

More often, they lose jobs because they saw the signals and convinced themselves the signals meant something else.

The layoff often starts twelve to twenty-four months before the HR meeting.

It starts when fewer junior hires are brought in, and when promotions begin slowing. When cross-functional teams quietly get smaller. When dashboards replace local judgment. When software absorbs first-pass thinking. When the same headcount is expected to manage far more output.

But because the paycheck still arrives, most workers mistake continuity for protection.

They confuse busyness with value.

They confuse praise with the future.

They confuse the title with the trajectory.

This is the head-in-the-sand stage.

Not stupidity.

Emotional self-protection.

Workers tell themselves:

This is just another software upgrade.

Management always talks about efficiency.

My field is different.

They still need people.

AI cannot do the human part.

The company values my experience.

This will level out.

Those thoughts are understandable.

They protect emotional stability in the short term.

But they can quietly destroy strategic mobility.

The most dangerous part is that the early stage of compression often feels positive.

Less repetitive work.

Smarter dashboards.

Faster workflows.

Better metrics.

More praise for output gains.

The worker interprets this as growth.

But sometimes the company is not preparing the worker for promotion.

It is preparing the workflow for consolidation.

That is why the final Friday HR meeting feels so shocking.

The worker thinks the story is about recognition.

The company knows the story has become about role reduction.

The family cost of denial is not only job loss.

It is lost time.

Every month spent pretending the change is temporary is a month not spent upgrading skills, learning AI workflows, building side leverage, protecting income, or repositioning toward resilient work.

The families that adapt fastest are not the ones who panic.

They are the ones who notice subtraction while the paycheck still exists.

They lift their heads before the sand hardens around them.

Reading the Tea Leaves Before the Meeting

Now imagine the same high performer from earlier.

Same school.

Same top company.

Same glowing reviews.

Same disappearing task layer.

But this time, he notices the pattern early.

He sees fewer junior hires coming in. He notices dashboards replacing the reports he once built manually. AI now drafts the first pass of customer communication, route planning, coding logic, and bookkeeping review. Senior leadership keeps using the same words in meetings: optimization, consolidation, efficiency gains, and integration.

He does not panic.

He translates.

He understands something many workers miss:

When the workflow gets easier, the role can become thinner.

The paycheck still exists, but the future may already be narrowing.

So he starts reading the tea leaves.

Instead of defending routine work, he moves closer to the work AI cannot own:

Judgment.

Exception handling.

Systems implementation.

Decision-making.

Human relationships.

Cross-team leadership.

He learns the AI tools directly, not casually, but as part of his workflow.

At night, while the paycheck still arrives, he takes classes on AI, workflow design, prompt strategy, systems integration, and adjacent skills that increase his market value.

He begins networking quietly with contacts at other companies.

Former coworkers.

Vendors.

Industry peers.

People in adjacent roles are growing instead of shrinking.

This is where a timeless truth pays off.

Early in my career, I truly worked like an old West hired gun. If you needed quick and positive results, I was your person. I enjoyed the pay, and if I'm honest, I enjoyed the boost it gave my ego.

But over time, I realized results alone were not enough.

Results can make you valuable. Relationships make you portable.

That realization changed everything.

I studied relationship building with the same intensity I once gave to execution. I learned that at the top levels of any company that matters, it is not only what you know, but also who knows you, trusts you, and believes in what you can build.

I developed relationships so strong that when great people moved to other job opportunities, they often took me with them. Better divisions. Bigger opportunities. More responsibility. Those doors opened because trust traveled faster than paperwork.

In the AI era, this principle becomes even more valuable. Build strong relationships with your bosses, vendors, Corporate Team and industry recruiters. Network endlessly, and spend dedicated time to prepare for your future. Always have other employment opportunities in your pocket like a full wallet. If needed, you have a well-planned job pivot strategy.

When skills get automated.

Workflows get compressed.

But trusted human relationships still create the bridge to the next opportunity before the market sees it.

Relationships turn uncertainty into intelligence.

And intelligence gives the worker speed.

While others are waiting for HR to define their future, he is already seeing where the next ladder is forming.

He starts looking at other jobs online.

Not because he is panicking.

Because optionality creates confidence.

He studies job descriptions, notices which AI skills keep appearing, and quietly prepares to pivot before the pressure makes every decision emotional.

The Friday HR meeting may still come.

But when it does, the story changes.

It hurts.

But it does not destroy the family.

Because the severance is no longer the beginning of panic.

It is the activation point of a pivot already in motion.

This is what smart workers and smart families do.

They do not wait for the formal ending.

They respond to the invisible beginning.

This is how you beat AI.

You do not fight the machine.

You learn it faster than the person next to you.

You use it to increase your speed, sharpen your judgment, widen your network, and create opportunities before the old ones disappear.

AI should not be the thing that takes your future.

It should be the tool that helps you take control of it.

This is how working families protect income, preserve dignity, and continue building the American Dream in a world that rewards leverage over routine.

Example of preparation to win and reading the Tea Leaves

Two hikers are walking through the woods when they suddenly come face to face with a huge bear.

One hiker immediately drops his backpack, pulls out a pair of running shoes, and starts lacing them up.

The other hiker says, "What are you doing? You can't outrun a bear."

The first hiker stands up and says, **"I don't have to outrun the bear. I just have to outrun you."**

Chapter 4:
The Middle Is Collapsing

"We used to have the strongest and most vibrant middle class on Earth. Not anymore. Today, 60% of our people are living paycheck to paycheck, and we have more income and wealth inequality than any other major country. Despite huge advances in technology and worker productivity, real weekly wages for the average American worker are lower today than they were 53 years ago." - Bernie Sanders.

The greatest danger to the American worker is not sudden unemployment.

It is compression.

Most people imagine economic disruption as something dramatic.

Factories close.

Mass layoffs hit the news.

Entire departments vanish overnight.

That does happen.

But more often, the middle collapses quietly.

The system does not remove everyone at once.

It tightens.

Entry-level roles shrink.

Mid-skill tasks get automated.

Output expectations rise.

Headcount growth slows.

Promotions flatten.

The middle does not explode.

It thins.

And thinning is harder to see than collapse.

Imagine standing in a hallway that slowly narrows.

At first, you barely notice.

There is still room to move. Still room to breathe. Still enough space to believe the future will widen again.

But over time, the walls begin moving inward.

Fewer openings appear.

Promotions take longer.

Raises flatten.

The competition at your level quietly doubles.

The same manager now oversees twice the territory.

The same analyst team now supports three departments instead of one.

The hallway narrows so gradually that many workers mistake it for normal career difficulty.

That is what compression feels like.

The danger is not always the disappearance of the role.

It is the shrinking of what the role can become.

This is especially dangerous in the modern American middle.

For decades, the middle class was built through:

- supervisory roles
- district operations
- office administration
- junior management
- regional logistics
- mid-level sales
- customer success leadership
- bookkeeping and finance support
- business analysts
- early IT systems roles

These jobs were created:

- predictable raises
- middle-income dignity
- home ownership
- stable tax bases
- school funding
- local business spending
- upward mobility for the next generation

AI does not always eliminate these roles.

It compresses them.

One regional manager now handles what once required three.

A single AI-assisted analyst now produces the output of an old five-person reporting team.

Customer service leaders inherit AI-routing systems that reduce headcount beneath them.

A logistics director now relies on software that removes layers of dispatch coordination.

The title still exists.

The ladder beneath it weakens.

This is why the middle is so vulnerable.

The middle historically depended on **routine plus moderate judgment**.

That combination was once the sweet spot of the American Dream.

Not executive-level power.

Not hourly fragility.

The middle.

But AI is uniquely capable of absorbing the routine side while amplifying the judgment side for fewer people.

That means the same amount of work can now flow upward into fewer hands.

This creates the quiet squeeze.

Workers feel it as:

- more responsibility without proportional pay
- wider territory without support layers

- stronger metrics but flatter raises
- more software, fewer people
- busier calendars, weaker bargaining power

And because the paycheck still arrives, most people do not call it compression.

They call it:

- a tougher market
- a demanding season
- temporary restructuring
- higher expectations
- doing more with less

But over time, the family feels it.

Raises no longer keep pace with housing.

College savings slow.

The second income becomes less optional.

The side business becomes a necessity.

Retirement contributions flatten.

The tax base in communities softens because middle-income growth slows.

This is where the American Dream begins to feel further away, even for hardworking families.

The danger is not only income pressure.

It is psychological narrowing.

A worker in a compressed middle often remains employed while slowly losing:

- bargaining power
- promotion visibility
- role mobility
- geographic flexibility
- confidence in the next ten years

That uncertainty bleeds into family decisions.

Do we move?

Can we afford a better school district?

Should we delay college plans?

Do we take the safer vacation?

Can we still start the business we talked about?

Compression changes household psychology long before it changes tax filings.

This is why the middle matters so much.

The middle is not just an income bracket.

It is the operating engine of the American Dream.

When the middle thins, the country feels it in:

- home ownership rates
- birth rates
- school quality
- local entrepreneurship

- municipal budgets
- long-term optimism

This is where the stakes rise beyond the individual household.

In my first book, I made a point that matters even more now: you owe your country your best effort to pursue the American Dream.

Soldiers bled and died so ordinary American families could have the right to build something better than what they inherited.

The middle class that emerged from that sacrifice became the tax base, the small-business engine, the school-funding backbone, and the long-term optimism that made America economically powerful.

If the middle collapses, we will not only lose jobs.

We are weakening the very structure generations fought to build.

That is why the answer is not fear.

It is mastery.

A complete understanding of AI, combined with the discipline to develop pivot strategies before everybody else does, is now part of what it means to protect the American Dream.

The next middle class will not be built by those who deny the technology.

It will be built by those who learn it early enough to use it for leverage, ownership, and family resilience.

The solution is not denial.

It is repositioning.

The workers and families who protect themselves from middle compression move toward:

- AI-assisted management
- exception-heavy decision roles
- ownership
- client trust
- trade + tech hybrids
- systems leadership
- relationship-driven business development
- entrepreneurial leverage

The goal is to move from being squeezed by the middle to **owning the systems the middle now depends on**.

That is the new upward mobility.

The middle is collapsing.

But collapse creates edges.

And the prepared worker learns to build on the edge before everyone else realizes the hallway is narrowing.

The goal now is to move from being squeezed by the middle to owning the systems the middle now depends on.

This is where awareness becomes an advantage. Once a worker understands that AI is compressing the middle, fear begins to lose its grip. Awareness gives families something most of the market does not yet have: time. And in every economic shift, time is the greatest asset a family can possess.

The average American does not need to become a software engineer to win in the AI era. That myth keeps too many good people frozen. The real opportunity is far more practical. The workers who achieve the American Dream in this next cycle will be the ones who learn how AI changes the flow of value in their industry, then position themselves one step closer to ownership, trust, and decision-making.

For some, that means becoming the person inside a company who knows how to use AI to remove waste, improve reporting, speed up customer response, or increase sales conversion. The worker who once followed systems can become the worker who now designs better systems. That shift changes bargaining power, compensation, and career durability.

For others, the opportunity sits outside traditional employment. AI now gives ordinary Americans leverage that once belonged only to large companies. A solo entrepreneur can use AI to build marketing campaigns, customer follow-up systems, research pipelines, bookkeeping support, and lead generation processes at a fraction of the old cost. A one-person business can now operate with the reach of a ten-person office if the owner learns how to direct the tools correctly.

This is how side income becomes wealth-building. A school administrator can build an AI-assisted consulting business helping districts streamline communication. A logistics coordinator can launch a freight optimization advisory firm. A former customer service leader can build AI-enhanced training systems for small businesses. A skilled tradesman can combine field expertise with AI quoting, scheduling, and follow-up systems to dominate local markets.

The American Dream has always belonged to the people who learned how value was shifting before the crowd did. AI simply accelerates the speed of that shift.

The families who win will treat AI as a force multiplier for discipline, not as a substitute for discipline. They will use it to reclaim time, reduce wasted effort, and redirect energy into assets that compound. That means building a business instead of only protecting a paycheck, creating digital products and services, buying into ownership roles faster, moving toward revenue responsibility, and teaching their children to use AI as a tool for leverage instead of a distraction.

This is where the American Dream becomes larger than survival. Home ownership, savings, investing, entrepreneurship, better schools, stronger communities, and family resilience all become more achievable when AI is used to multiply output instead of threatening identity.

The average American should think in three moves. First, use AI to become dramatically better at your current work. Second, use the time and confidence that creates to build a second layer of income, expertise, or ownership. Third, convert higher income into durable American Dream assets: a home, investments, education, business equity, and family opportunity.

That is the real pivot. AI is not the end of upward mobility. For the prepared worker, it can become the greatest expansion of upward mobility in a generation. The families who preserve the American Dream will be the ones who pivot before everyone else finally admits the walls are closing in.

A few words about Complacency – let it be your mortal enemy!

Complacency is the most dangerous enemy facing the American worker in the AI era, not because it is loud, but because it is silent. It does not arrive with warning sirens, pink slips, or headlines announcing that your position is gone tomorrow morning. It arrives as comfort. It whispers that your experience is enough, that your company needs you, that the way things have always been done will somehow continue. That lie has destroyed more careers than incompetence ever will.

For generations, American workers were taught that loyalty, consistency, and hard work created security. For a long time, that was mostly true. If you showed up early, mastered your craft, and gave your employer your best years, there was a reasonable expectation that your future would remain stable. But AI has changed the speed of business so dramatically that stability itself has become temporary. The systems being deployed today do not replace entire companies overnight. They replace tasks first, then workflows, then departments, and finally careers. By the time the average worker notices what is happening, the economic momentum has already shifted underneath them.

That is why complacency is so deadly. It convinces good people to mistake today's paycheck for tomorrow's protection.

The American worker cannot afford to confuse being employed with being secure.

In this era, security no longer comes from the title on your business card. It comes from your ability to learn faster than the systems changing around you. It comes from your willingness to study the tools that may one day threaten your role and then master them before someone else does. The worker who says, "AI does not affect my industry," is often the same worker who wakes up one Friday morning to discover half their daily responsibilities now happen automatically through software they barely noticed being installed.

The danger is not just job loss. The danger is becoming economically irrelevant while still believing you are safe.

Every American worker should treat complacency as the enemy because complacency kills urgency, and urgency is now a professional survival skill. The workers who will preserve their place in the middle class, build wealth, and continue chasing the American Dream are not necessarily the smartest people in the room. They are the ones who remain alert. They read the signals early. They notice when fewer people are being hired. They recognize when software begins taking over repetitive tasks. They pay attention when management starts measuring productivity in ways that favor automation. They do not dismiss these signals as temporary noise. They move.

This is where the bear story becomes more than a joke. In this economy, you do not need to outrun every technological advancement. You simply need to outrun complacency. You need to move before the average worker moves. Learn AI tools before your department mandates them. Build relationships before your company restructures. Develop a side income before your salary comes under pressure. Position yourself where judgment, leadership, trust, and human connection still matter.

The workers who lose are often not the least capable. They are the ones who waited too long because comfort felt safer than preparation.

Complacency also destroys something deeper than income. It erodes personal confidence. When people wait until a disruption is public, they are forced to react emotionally instead of strategically. Fear replaces planning. Pride delays pivots. Families lose financial momentum because the decision to adapt came months or years too late. In contrast, the worker who treats complacency as the enemy stays in motion. They are constantly adding skills, expanding networks, understanding new systems, and looking around corners. That movement creates confidence because they know they are building options before options are required.

This is the new American responsibility in the AI era. The men and women who want to protect their families, preserve their dignity, and continue building the American Dream must become students of change. The goal is not panic. Panic creates paralysis. The goal is disciplined awareness followed by decisive action.

The middle class will not be saved by nostalgia for how work used to be. It will be preserved by workers who refuse to become comfortable while the world is changing around them.

In the years ahead, complacency will quietly destroy millions of careers. But for the worker who decides today to stay sharp, move early, and master the tools of the future, AI becomes less of a threat and more of a lever.

That is how you beat the bear.

Not by pretending it is not there.

By running before everyone else hears it coming.

Chapter 5

The Families Who Teach AI Early Will Own the Future

The next American Dream will not belong only to the workers who adapt.

It will belong to the families who adapt together.

When I was twelve years old, my father sat me down and gave me one of the most important lessons of my life.

He told me I needed to always try to be the best at everything I chose to do. He said in our Country. I could blaze my own trail, and there was no limit to what I could achieve.

If I studied, worked tirelessly, and set lofty goals, I could do and become anything.

What he was really teaching me was bigger than motivation.

He was teaching me that this country constantly evolves, constantly changes, and that greatness belongs to those who adapt without lowering their standards.

I do not believe I disappointed him.

But this is where we are today with the coming of AI.

The principle has not changed.

The tools have.

What fathers once passed down as grit, discipline, and belief must now also include the ability to use AI as leverage.

The families who understand this early will not fear the future.

They will help build it.

For generations, strong families passed down the tools of upward mobility in forms that matched their era.

They passed down discipline.

Work ethic.

Faith.

Patience.

Craftsmanship.

The belief that tomorrow could be better than today.

Those values still matter.

But in the AI era, they are no longer enough by themselves.

The family that adds AI fluency to those values will widen opportunity in ways previous generations could barely imagine.

This is not about turning children into coders.

This is about teaching children how to think with tools that multiply research, communication, creativity, and execution.

The child who learns this early will move through school, work, and entrepreneurship with leverage that compounds for decades.

The education system is already behind.

But families must also be honest about their own role in how unprepared many children have become.

Too many parents have floated along when it comes to their child's education.

Parent-teacher conferences became optional, then replaced by quick emails, skimmed updates, and the illusion that passive awareness equals active parenting.

It does not.

At the same time, too many children have been allowed to drift into comfort without challenge: overweight, isolated, locked into gaming worlds, and increasingly unable to communicate confidently with adults, mentors, customers, or future employers.

That has to change if we want our children to have a real shot at the American Dream.

If you asked a room full of tenth graders what the American Dream means, most would struggle to answer.

That is not only a school problem.

It is a family doctrine problem.

Children cannot pursue what has never been clearly defined for them.

Families must once again teach what upward mobility means: discipline, communication, ownership, resilience, health, responsibility, and now AI leverage.

Children must learn how to communicate like educated adults at an early stage.

In an AI-driven world, clear speaking, strong writing, eye contact, confidence, and the ability to hold thoughtful conversations with adults will separate leaders from followers.

They also need to understand leadership itself.

Leadership means taking responsibility, making decisions under pressure, serving others, setting standards, and being the person others trust when the path is unclear.

That means parents must deliberately teach:

1. How to ask better questions
2. How to verify AI outputs against reality
3. How to turn time savings into asset creation
4. How to build a side income before lifestyle inflation
5. How to combine human trust with machine speed
6. How to communicate with confidence
7. How to lead when others hesitate

This is where the family dinner table changes.

Previous generations asked children what they learned in school.

The new question becomes:

What did you build with what you learned today?

That shift moves a family from passive education to active leverage.

Instead of raising children to become applicants, families begin raising builders.

A sixteen-year-old who learns to use AI for local lead generation can help neighborhood businesses get customers.

A college student can build AI-assisted tutoring services.

A young tradesperson can use AI quoting, scheduling, and customer follow-up to outgrow older competitors.

A future real estate professional can analyze neighborhoods, draft listings, and automate follow-up while competitors still work manually.

The advantage is not the software.

The advantage is early familiarity.

Confidence compounds.

Children who grow up seeing AI as a tool for leverage will move faster toward ownership, revenue, and independence.

This is where the American Dream becomes generational again.

The old dream was often one generation sacrificing so the next could have a safer job.

The new dream is one generation teaching the next how to create leverage so they never depend on a single fragile path.

The families who wait will still have an opportunity.

But it is also the responsibility of the family to instill something deeper than opportunity: patriotic duty.

Every American child should understand that the freedom to pursue the American Dream was protected by soldiers who gave the ultimate sacrifice so future generations could build lives larger than what they inherited.

That freedom is not abstract.

It is a birthright paid for by courage, discipline, and sacrifice. And because it was paid for so dearly, it should be honored, not squandered.

Families must teach children that pursuing excellence is not only personal ambition. It is a way of respecting the generations who defended the nation and preserved the right to rise.

The families who teach AI early will own the future because they will produce children who enter adulthood already understanding leverage.

They will not simply seek employment. They will seek systems, ownership, clients, audiences, and assets.

That is the next version of the American Dream. Not just a better paycheck. A better starting position for every generation that follows.

The families who start now will own the learning curve.

And in every major economic shift, the people who own the learning curve eventually own the outcome.

Chapter 6

The 777 Doctrine

Learn. Earn. Own. Repeat.

Why the First 777 Days Decide Who Survives the AI Economy?

The first 777 days after high school, trade school, college, military service, or a major career pivot now carry extraordinary weight.

In previous generations, people had more time to drift, recover from bad first choices, and slowly work their way into the right lane.

That world is disappearing.

AI compresses learning curves, rewards early reputation, and accelerates the separation between those who move with intention and those who simply hope stability finds them.

The first 777 days are where momentum is either built or quietly surrendered.

1) Why Your First Move Matters More Now

Your first move matters because the market is changing faster than institutions can explain it.

A strong first move places you near growth, decision-making, and evolving systems.

A weak first move often traps you inside routine work that becomes easier to automate.

In the AI economy, speed of adaptation compounds.

The person who learns modern tools, builds proof of work (portfolio), and develops confidence in the first 777 days gains an advantage that multiplies for years.

They are promoted sooner, trusted earlier, and given access to larger decisions.

The opposite is also true.

A young worker who spends the first 777 days in passive roles, waiting for instructions and collecting generic experience, may discover that the market has already moved beyond what they spent years learning.

The lesson is simple:

Do not optimize for comfort.

Optimize for learning velocity, exposure, and compounding trust.

2) Choose Proximity to Revenue

The smartest early-career decision is to get close to the money flow.

Revenue teaches reality.

It reveals what customers value, what companies protect, and what leaders notice.

That means choosing roles tied to:

- sales
- business development
- customer acquisition
- account growth

- operations tied to margin
- logistics optimization
- AI systems that improve output
- leadership tracks connected to measurable business outcomes

When you are close to revenue, your work becomes visible.

Visible work creates leverage.

Leverage creates options.

Even technical workers should think this way.

The engineer who understands how their system affects margin will rise faster than the engineer who only understands code.

The analyst who ties dashboards to profit decisions becomes far harder to replace.

In the first 777 days, the goal is not to collect titles.

It is to learn where value enters the business and how you can multiply it.

3) Do Not Chase Titles, Chase Leverage

Too many people waste early years chasing status labels that sound impressive but create no real control over their future.

The AI economy punishes vanity and rewards leverage.

Leverage means skills and positioning that continue paying you after the immediate task is done.

That includes:

- trusted relationships
- client access
- repeatable systems
- process ownership
- AI workflows
- audience building
- digital proof of work
- deal flow

A modest role with real access to decision-makers is often worth far more than a prestigious title buried under layers of bureaucracy.

The right question in the first 777 days is not "Does this sound impressive?"

It is:

"Will this give me compounding control, visibility, and optionality?"

Leverage always outlasts prestige.

4) Build Your Reputation Digitally

In the AI economy, your digital footprint is part of your professional equity.

A résumé is static.

A reputation ecosystem compounds.

Every young professional should use the first 777 days to build visible proof of competence:

- a strong LinkedIn presence
- thoughtful industry posts
- case studies
- before-and-after business results
- AI workflow experiments
- writing samples
- short-form videos explaining insights
- public project breakdowns

This is not ego.

It is discoverability.

Most people lose long before they realize the game has started.

That is the real danger of the AI economy.

It is not the layoff meeting. It is not the Friday calendar invite from HR. It is not the polite severance package slid across the table by someone reading from a script.

The real loss happens in the **months and years before the disruption becomes visible**.

It happens in the quiet moments when people tell themselves they still have time.

Next quarter. Next year. After the kids are older. After the market settles. After leadership makes its move. After they feel "ready."

But readiness is rarely what creates survival. Discipline does.

The workers, families, and entrepreneurs who win the next decade are not necessarily smarter than everyone else. They simply begin earlier, move with more intention, and stay committed long enough for compounding to take over.

That is why I want to give you a framework that can guide every pivot you make for the rest of your life:

The 777-Day Rule.

For any meaningful reinvention, business launch, skill transition, industry pivot, or AI adaptation strategy, the first **777 days** will decide more than the next 10 years.

That sounds dramatic, but history keeps proving it.

The market rewards visible success. Reality rewards invisible preparation.

And in the age of AI, invisible preparation is everything.

The Worker Who Waited

Picture a mid-career operations manager named Steve.

For twelve years, he built a stable career coordinating schedules, vendor communications, internal reporting, and process improvement. He was good at what he did. Reliable. Trusted. The kind of employee companies describe as "valuable" right up until software can do 60 percent of the role.

The signs were there.

New AI reporting dashboards. Automated vendor routing. Meeting summaries are generated instantly. Forecasting tools, leadership suddenly loved.

He saw it.

He even talked about it over lunch.

"AI is coming for a lot of jobs."

He said the right words. What he did not do was move.

He spent 18 months consuming headlines instead of building leverage. He watched videos but never learned the tools. He worried but never experimented. He stayed loyal to a company that was already modeling a future without his position.

By the time the role was consolidated, he was entering the market at the same time as thousands of others were doing the same thing.

That is what waiting does. It pushes you into competition at the exact moment everyone else is panicking.

People love synchronized fear. It's one of our least efficient hobbies.

The Worker Who Started Early

Now picture someone else.

Maria worked in a similar environment and saw the same signals. But instead of treating the warning signs like background noise, she started her **777-day clock**.

In the first 90 days, she studied prompt design, workflow automation, meeting summarization, CRM augmentation, and AI-assisted client reporting.

By day 180, she was the person on her team showing others how to cut five hours of repetitive work into twenty minutes.

By day 300, leadership was asking for her input on process redesign.

By day 500, she had built a side consulting income helping local businesses integrate AI into customer operations.

By day 777, she no longer depended on one employer for survival.

The same technology that threatened average workers became the exact tool that multiplied her value.

This is the central lesson of this chapter:

AI punishes hesitation and rewards early systems thinking.

Days 1-100: Research Before Results

The first hundred days are frustrating because they rarely produce applause.

This is where weak people quit. Not because the strategy is wrong, but because the scoreboard is still blank.

Days 1 through 100 are for:

- learning the landscape
- identifying which parts of your industry are repetitive
- testing AI tools daily
- reading labor signals
- watching where budgets are moving
- finding where humans still create judgment, trust, and accountability

This is where you build your map.

The average person mistakes a lack of immediate reward for a lack of progress. That mistake destroys careers.

Your first hundred days are supposed to feel slow. This is reconnaissance.

No soldier storms a battlefield without studying the terrain. Don't casually hand your future to whatever mood your employer is in that quarter.

Days 100-300: Identity Shift

This is where the transformation gets personal.

By now, the issue is no longer information. The issue is identity.

Do you still see yourself as the old version of who you were?

The administrative assistant. The junior analyst. The dispatcher. The call center supervisor. The entry-level coder.

Or are you becoming a **systems thinker who uses AI to amplify outcomes**?

This stretch is where confidence is built through repetition.

You stop dabbling. You start integrating.

Every day should include one act of deliberate leverage:

- automate one task
- improve one workflow
- Write one public insight
- build one relationship
- document one learning
- Create one asset that compounds later

The point is not speed. The point is momentum.

Once identity shifts, discipline becomes easier because the work is no longer something you "try." It becomes who you are.

Days 300-500: Proof of Traction

This is where the outside world finally starts seeing what you have been building.

Opportunities begin to show up.

People ask for help. Managers notice. Peers seek guidance. Clients start paying. Followers begin sharing your content. Your name enters rooms before you do.

This phase matters because evidence kills doubt.

What felt invisible in the first 300 days now starts to compound into measurable proof.

This is why most people misunderstand success. They see visible traction and assume it happened fast.

It did not happen fast. It happened quietly.

The market simply noticed late.

That delay between effort and recognition is where fortunes are made.

Days 500-777: Market Separation

This is where the disciplined become impossible to ignore.

By this point, your skill stack should include:

- AI fluency in your field
- industry-specific judgment
- network credibility

- audience trust
- a second income path
- a documented reputation
- the ability to pivot faster than your peers

Now the market separates.

People who waited are just beginning to feel fear. You are already executing.

People who stayed passive are reading headlines. You are monetizing capability.

People who still think loyalty is a strategy are discovering the spreadsheet logic of modern corporations. You are building portability.

That is what day 777 represents.

Not perfection.

Strategic irreversibility.

You have become too adaptive to be easily broken.

The American Dream Requires a Time Horizon

This book has been direct about one thing from the beginning: no institution is coming to protect your future.

But that does not mean the American Dream is dead.

It means the Dream now belongs to people willing to **operate with discipline over time**.

The generations before us honored sacrifice through work, grit, and responsibility. Men stormed beaches, flew bombers, built highways, stocked grocery shelves, ran routes, worked plants, and created the middle class brick by brick.

The modern version of that responsibility is different.

Today, honoring that inheritance means refusing complacency in the face of technological change.

It means learning faster. It means pivoting earlier. It means using AI before disruption forces your hand.

Freedom without responsibility decays. Opportunity without discipline disappears.

The Dream still belongs to those willing to earn it.

Your 777-Day Plan

I want the reader to leave this chapter with something practical.

Start your 777 days now. Not when fear arrives. Now.

Choose one of these:

1. Reinvent your current role with AI
2. Build a second income stream
3. Develop a niche authority platform
4. Create a business around a repetitive industry problem
5. Build AI fluency inside your current trade

Then commit to these non-negotiables:

- **Daily:** 30 minutes of learning and one applied action
- **Weekly:** publish one insight, meet one new person, improve one system

- **Monthly:** audit momentum, revenue, leverage, and market demand
- **Quarterly:** eliminate what is not compounding
- **Annually:** compare yourself to where you were 365 days ago, not to someone else's chapter 20

The goal is simple: become more valuable to the future every single week.

Closing Punch

The future will not be won by the most naturally talented.

It will be won by the people who respected the compounding power of early action.

The market always looks sudden from the outside.

But collapse and success are both usually the result of **hundreds of quiet days no one else saw**.

That is why your first 777 days matter.

They decide whether AI becomes your layoff notice or your launch platform.

They decide whether your family inherits fear or momentum.

They decide whether you spend the next decade reacting to change or leading it.

Because by the time panic reaches the crowd, the winners are already too far ahead to catch.

And in this economy, the people who move first do not just survive. They own the future.

Buy Time before Lifestyle Inflation

One of the greatest strategic mistakes in the first 777 days is increasing lifestyle costs before building durable leverage.

A nicer apartment, expensive car payment, status purchases, and avoidable debt can trap a young worker in fragile career decisions.

The disciplined move is to buy time.

Keep expenses low.

Protect mobility.

Create margin in your life.

Time margin allows you to:

- leave bad industries faster
- Invest in new skills
- take strategic risks
- start side businesses
- Relocate toward opportunity
- survive instability for long-term gain

This is where the American Dream begins to separate into two paths.

One group spends early income proving success.

The other uses early income to buy freedom, assets, and future choices.

The second group usually wins.

6) The American Dream 777-Day Doctrine

The doctrine for the first 777 days is simple:

Learn. Earn. Own. Repeat.

Learn faster than your peers.

Master AI tools, communication, leadership, and the economics of your industry.

Earn through visible contribution.

Move toward revenue, trusted execution, and measurable results.

Own as early as possible.

That ownership may be business equity, commission upside, investments, real estate, content assets, or a side company.

The form matters less than the principle:

Convert labor into assets.

Then repeat the cycle at a higher level.

Each loop should move you further from pure time-for-money dependency and closer to systems, ownership, and family security.

In the AI economy, the first 777 days are not an introduction.

They are the foundation your future family will stand on.

The people who use this period wisely will not simply build careers.

They will build dynasties of opportunity.

This is where laser focus matters. Every hour spent in the first 300 days should increase leverage for what follows. Reading should sharpen judgment. Research should reduce avoidable mistakes. Conversations should shorten the learning curve. Execution should be tied to milestones, not moods.

To make the 777-day doctrine practical, the first **300 days** of any serious 777-day build must become **sacred**. This is where most projects, careers, businesses, books, and family pivots either gain momentum or quietly die from distraction.

The 777-day program should become a major doctrine of this book: The first 300 days are for clarity, systems, and positioning. The next 477 days are for scale, ownership, and compounding returns.

- *I did not choose 777 because of superstition, luck, or numerology.*

I chose it because it is long enough to force transformation, short enough to demand urgency, and memorable enough that families

can build discipline around it.

Chapter 7

The Family, AI-Proof

How Households Build an AI-Proof Future Before the Market Breaks Them

When I was ten years old, my family faced a crisis that I would not fully understand until much later in life.

At the time, my father worked for Safeway Grocery Stores. He had built his career there through discipline, consistency, and the kind of loyalty that used to mean something in corporate America. To a ten-year-old boy, Safeway felt permanent. Grocery stores were always there. The lights were always on. The shelves were always full. My father's job felt as solid as the building itself.

Then the closures began.

One by one, Safeway started shutting down stores across our area.

Most people around us treated it like temporary turbulence. They assumed the company would stabilize, that the closures would stop, or that somehow their own location would be spared.

My father did not think that way.

He studied the pattern. He looked at the decisions leadership was making. He listened to the conversations happening behind the scenes. And then he made a hard assessment:

Within 18 months, he believed he would be out of a job.

That realization did not send him into panic. It sent him into leadership.

One night after dinner, he called a family meeting.

It was my father, my mother, my brother, and me sitting together, talking through the future like a small leadership team long before I had words for what that meant.

He laid out the reality in clear terms. The company was closing stores. The odds were getting worse. The future in our State no longer looked stable.

Then he did something that shaped the way I would think about crisis for the rest of my life.

He made the family part of the strategy.

We discussed every realistic option.

Do we move to another state and follow the company? Do we stay in our hometown and prepare for the worst? What expenses can we reduce now? How do we protect the family if the closures continue?

Nothing about that conversation felt dramatic. It felt disciplined.

Looking back, that may have been the first masterclass I ever received in strategic thinking under pressure.

The decision was made to stay.

We loved our town, our routines, our community, and the life we had built there. So instead of reacting emotionally, my parents chose preparation.

Our family tightened its expenses. We conserved money. We cut back where we could. There was a seriousness in the house, but never chaos.

My father, meanwhile, began exploring every professional option available to him.

He did not wait for the final closure notice. He did not trust hope as a strategy. He started building relationships, talking to contacts, and leaning into the network he had developed through years of trust and credibility.

Then the day came.

Safeway closed every remaining location in the state.

The crisis he had predicted arrived almost exactly on schedule.

But because he had moved early, our family was not caught flat-footed.

Through the relationships he had built, he transitioned into a new role with a major grocery distributor as a **Distribution Representative**.

The company changed. The title changed. The future changed.

But because he had prepared before the crowd panicked, our family's trajectory remained intact.

That lesson stayed with me.

The real power was never the job itself. It was my father's ability to read weak signals early, involve the family in reality, conserve resources before the emergency, and use relationships as a bridge into the next opportunity.

That is not just a childhood memory.

It is a blueprint.

In today's AI economy, workers and families face the same kind of moment. The names of the companies are different. The technology is different. The speed is faster. But the principle is exactly the same.

The people who survive disruption are rarely the people who wait for certainty.

They are the people who recognize the pattern early, gather the family, reduce unnecessary risk, build options, and move before the final closure sign goes up.

My father taught me that long before AI existed.

Crisis does not destroy families. **Delay does.**

The first place disruption is rarely felt in the office.

It is the kitchen table.

It is the silence between a husband and wife after the kids go to bed. It is a glance at the mortgage statement. It is the quiet math of tuition, groceries, car payments, and retirement accounts. It is the moment a parent realizes the advice they gave their children may no longer match the world those children are walking into.

That is where this chapter truly begins.

Because careers may collapse at work, but the consequences always land at home.

The families who survive the AI economy will not be the ones with the highest incomes. They will be the ones with the strongest doctrine.

A household without a doctrine drifts. A drifting family mistakes yesterday's rules for tomorrow's protection.

That mistake is becoming expensive.

The Kitchen-Table Realization

Picture a father who spent twenty years climbing into middle management.

He did everything the old system rewarded. He earned trust. He stayed loyal. He worked late. He became dependable.

Then, one quarter, leadership rolls out new AI planning systems, automated reporting, and predictive workforce tools. Six months later, his division is restructured. A year later, his role disappears.

The real pain is not only the lost paycheck.

It is the realization that for years, he taught his children the same rules that just failed him:

- go to school
- Get a stable job
- work hard
- stay loyal
- Wait for your turn

For decades, that advice built the middle class. Today, in many industries, it can become an inherent fragility.

That is the moment the family must decide whether to cling to nostalgia or build a new doctrine.

People are strangely sentimental about broken maps. They'll frame them on the wall before admitting the road moved.

The Lies Families Still Repeat

The danger is not AI alone. The danger is outdated family language.

Families still repeat phrases that sound responsible but no longer guarantee resilience:

- "Just get a degree."
- "Find something stable."
- "The company will take care of you."
- "Benefits matter more than adaptability."
- "Once you get in somewhere good, you're set."

These ideas were not foolish in the industrial and corporate eras that created the modern middle class.

But in a world of task automation, AI copilots, synthetic candidates, and shrinking entry paths, these phrases are no longer enough.

The new family doctrine must teach something stronger:

Learn fast, build leverage, create portability, and never let one institution control your future.

The Anti-Fragile Household

An anti-fragile family does not merely survive pressure. It improves because of it.

That means every household needs four systems:

1. **A learning culture** Every family member should be growing a skill that compounds.
2. **Income redundancy** One paycheck is no longer enough protection in a rapidly shifting market.
3. **AI literacy** Every adult and every age-appropriate child should understand how AI changes work.
4. **Weekly strategic conversations** Families should talk openly about careers, risks, pivots, and new opportunities.

The strongest households in the next decade will act more like small strategic enterprises than passive consumers of whatever the economy hands them.

That may sound cold. It is actually freedom.

Raising Adaptive Children

Parents now carry a responsibility that previous generations did not.

It is no longer enough to prepare children for tests. You must prepare them for reinvention.

Children should grow up learning:

- systems thinking
- communication
- persuasion
- judgment
- creativity
- resilience
- AI collaboration
- problem framing
- relationship building

The future will reward people who can work with intelligent systems while still bringing human trust, leadership, and accountability.

Blind compliance will be cheap. Original thinking will not.

Reward curiosity. Reward initiative. Reward experimentation.

Teach children that failure in learning is tuition, not identity.

That is how you build confidence instead of dependence.

Marriage and Partnership as Strategic Alliance

In the old model, one spouse often carried the career burden while the other stabilized the home.

That model is changing.

Now both partners must think strategically about the future.

A strong marriage in the AI era means becoming allies in adaptation.

That includes:

- monthly skill audits
- household financial redundancy planning
- discussing industry threats early
- encouraging pivots before a crisis
- building second income channels
- supporting each other's learning curve

The best partnerships will not treat disruption like a private burden. They will treat it like a shared mission.

The household becomes the first boardroom.

The New American Dream Doctrine

This book has been clear that the American Dream still exists.

But it no longer belongs automatically to those who simply follow old instructions.

Today, patriotism inside the household means preparing your bloodline for the world that is actually coming.

The generations before us defended freedom with discipline, sacrifice, and work. The modern duty is to preserve that inheritance by refusing complacency.

A family that embraces learning, adapts early, and teaches courage in the face of change is not just protecting income.

It is defending legacy.

That is the new doctrine.

Closing Punch

The next generation will inherit more than your money.

They will inherit your beliefs about work. Your relationship with change. Your willingness to learn. Your courage under uncertainty.

They will inherit either your discipline or your denial.

And in the AI era, that difference may decide whether your family line expands the American Dream or spends decades trying to recover what hesitation destroyed.

Chapter 8

The Broken Pipeline

How Schools, Colleges, and Career Systems Still Prepare Students for Jobs That Are Already Disappearing

Every generation inherits a story about how success is supposed to work.

Go to school. Pick the right major. Get the degree. Start at the bottom. Work your way up.

For decades, that pipeline built careers, communities, and the middle class.

Today, too often, it delivers young people into debt, confusion, and shrinking entry points.

The problem is not education itself. The problem is that too many institutions are still preparing students for a labor market that has already moved.

By the time the curriculum catches up, the bottom rung is gone. That's the bureaucratic tragedy nobody wants to say out loud.

A Boat Mechanic With a Philosophy Degree

During the winter months, I spend time at my house in Marathon, Florida, right in the middle of the Keys.

It is one of my favorite places to think and write. The town is alive with movement: jet skis cutting across the water, boats heading to the sandbars, fishermen chasing the next bite, and some of the clearest ocean water you will ever see.

A couple of years ago, I had an issue with my boat and took it to the next Key over, where a mechanic worked out of his house doing small boat repairs.

After we talked through the repair, I asked him how he ended up building a life fixing boats in the Keys.

His answer stuck with me.

He told me he had earned a **degree in Philosophy** from Penn State University.

After graduation, he could not find meaningful work tied to that degree. No clear career track. No obvious ladder. No institutional bridge from classroom to livelihood.

So he pivoted.

Back in high school, he had worked in a small boat shop. He liked the work. He understood engines, fiberglass, wiring, and the practical side of problem-solving. So when the degree did not open doors, he fell back on a skill that actually created value.

Before long, he was building a life in the Keys doing something he genuinely enjoyed.

The lesson was not that Philosophy was useless. The lesson was that **somewhere along the line, no one helped him connect education to market reality**.

No parent stepped in with enough strategic pressure. No counselor mapped real outcomes. No institution forced the harder question:

What does this path look like in the real economy?

Yet the story also contains hope. Because he had a fallback skill, he was able to pivot into work he loved.

That is exactly what this chapter is about.

The modern danger is not choosing the wrong degree. It is building an identity around a path without preserving the ability to pivot.

The Guidance Gap

Too many students are still being guided by outdated assumptions.

The advice sounds responsible:

- follow your passion
- Get the credential
- build a résumé
- start anywhere
- Experience will protect you

But in many AI-exposed industries, the "start anywhere" jobs are disappearing first.

Customer support. Administrative coordination. Junior analysis. Entry-level coding. Basic bookkeeping. Scheduling. Research assistance.

These were once the proving grounds. Now they are often the first workflows absorbed by software.

That means the pipeline itself is broken.

Students are still being aimed at doors that may not exist by the time they arrive.

The Vanishing First Rung

One of the most dangerous failures in the modern education system is the refusal to acknowledge what is happening to **internships and entry-level jobs**.

For generations, these roles were the first rung of economic mobility.

Internships gave students proximity. They learned how offices worked. They built relationships. They made mistakes in lower-risk environments. They converted classroom theory into market reality.

Entry-level jobs did even more.

They were the proving grounds where young workers learned judgment, urgency, communication, systems, politics, and trust. No one started at the top. The bottom rung taught the rhythm of professional life.

That is exactly why this shift is so dangerous.

The bottom rung is disappearing first.

AI now drafts reports once handed to junior analysts. Automated systems answer customer-service requests once handled by first-year staff. Scheduling, bookkeeping, data cleanup, onboarding documentation, administrative coordination, and first-pass coding work are being absorbed into software layers before young workers ever touch them.

The tragedy is not just job loss.

It is **experience loss**.

When internships shrink and entry-level roles vanish, students are not merely losing income. They are losing the laboratory where competence used to be formed.

And yet too many high schools, colleges, and career offices still operate as if the old sequence remains untouched.

Students are still told:

- Get the degree
- land the internship
- start at the bottom
- prove yourself
- work your way up

But what happens when the bottom no longer exists?

What happens when the internship pool gets cut in half because software now handles the busywork that once justified bringing students in?

What happens when companies no longer need ten junior people because two senior people with AI tools can do the same output?

This is where institutional silence becomes dangerous.

Colleges continue marketing career paths built on assumptions from ten years ago. High schools still push résumé-building checklists without explaining that the early proving grounds are collapsing in real time.

Young people are being prepared for doors that may be locked before graduation.

That is not a student failure. That is a **pipeline design failure**.

The institutions responsible for launching careers are not moving fast enough to admit that the launchpad itself is changing shape.

The new first rung must become something different:

- project portfolios
- AI-assisted apprenticeships
- creator-led skill proof
- paid micro-consulting
- direct audience building
- Freelance system solving
- niche community authority
- trade plus tech hybrid skills

The future belongs to students who can **demonstrate leverage before permission is granted**.

Because waiting for the old internship-to-entry-job pipeline to save them may become the very thing that leaves them behind.

The Degree Illusion

A degree still has value. Let's not pretend otherwise.

It teaches discipline, exposure, critical thinking, and in many cases provides social proof.

But the dangerous illusion is believing the credential alone creates safety.

It does not.

What creates safety now is the combination of:

- adaptable skills
- AI fluency

- communication
- sales ability
- systems thinking
- relationship capital
- a fallback capability that creates immediate market value

That boat mechanic in Marathon had exactly that.

His fallback capability became his real leverage.

The degree shaped his mind. The practical skill protected his future.

That combination is what young people need now.

What Schools Should Really Teach

The schools and colleges that will matter in the next decade must teach students how to survive moving targets.

That means the new curriculum should include:

- AI collaboration
- prompt design
- systems thinking
- persuasion
- negotiation
- entrepreneurship
- audience building
- practical trades exposure
- financial literacy

- market mapping
- relationship building
- pivot planning

The old system trained people for fixed ladders. The new system must train people to move through terrain.

The winners will not be the students with the neatest résumés. They will be the ones who combine education with optionality, practical leverage, and the courage to pivot when reality refuses to honor the plan.

That's the deeper wound most people miss.

Young people are not only losing a paycheck. They are losing the **practice arena where judgment, urgency, politics, communication, and trust used to form**.

That's the line colleges and high schools are failing to acknowledge while still handing out résumé workshops like the floorboards aren't rotting beneath them.

The new replacement ladder section is the main message to you:

- portfolios
- AI apprenticeships
- micro-consulting
- audience building
- hybrid trade + tech skills

That gives you a rebuild path instead of just another funeral for the old system, and books need oxygen after hard truths, or people mentally check out and go scroll nonsense.

The College Student AI Survival Playbook

This book is not here to simply warn people. It is here to provide a roadmap.

So let's make this practical for every college student reading it.

If you are in college right now, you are entering the workforce during one of the fastest labor shifts in modern history. That is not bad news if you move early. It is only bad news if you keep following a map that assumes the old ladder is still there.

Here is what college students need to do now to be ready for AI.

1) Learn AI Before Your Professors Teach It

Do not wait for the curriculum to catch up. In many schools, by the time a formal AI class is approved, the workplace has already moved another year ahead.

Every student should be actively learning:

- prompt design
- workflow automation
- research acceleration
- data interpretation
- content drafting
- presentation building
- spreadsheet analysis
- AI-assisted coding
- customer workflow tools

The students who graduate already fluent in these systems will enter interviews with leverage instead of hope.

2) Build Proof, Not Just Credentials

The degree gets attention. Proof gets hired.

Build a portfolio that shows what you can actually do:

- AI-assisted case studies
- process improvement projects
- dashboards
- sales systems
- market research reports
- social audience growth
- automation workflows
- niche consulting samples

In the new market, employers and clients increasingly trust demonstrated outcomes over theoretical transcripts.

3) Combine Human Skills With AI Leverage

The safest students will not be the most technical. They will be the most difficult to replace.

That means combining AI fluency with deeply human advantages:

- communication
- persuasion
- leadership

- judgment
- relationship building
- negotiation
- storytelling
- decision-making under pressure

AI can generate options. Humans still win by choosing the right one.

4) Create Income Before Graduation

One of the smartest things a student can do today is generate some form of income before the diploma arrives.

That could be:

- freelance work
- paid content creation
- tutoring with AI support
- micro-consulting for local businesses
- trade work on weekends
- niche agency services
- campus-side entrepreneurship

The point is not the money alone. The point is learning how the market rewards value.

That lesson will matter more than many elective credits.

5) Build Relationships Across Generations

Students often make the mistake of networking only with peers. That is too small.

Build relationships with:

- professors who understand industry
- local business owners
- alumni
- trade professionals
- founders
- operators
- managers already using AI

Career acceleration increasingly happens through trusted introductions, not blind applications.

6) Preserve the Ability to Pivot

Do not build your identity around one title before you have even entered the market.

The world is moving too fast for rigid career identity.

Build skills that travel:

- sales
- systems
- writing
- analytics
- leadership

- automation
- trade capability
- digital distribution

The goal is simple: no matter what changes, you always have a way to create value.

That is how students stop fearing AI and start using it as leverage.

The students who thrive will not be the ones who wait for permission. They will be the ones who treated college as a launchpad for adaptability.

Closing Punch

The tragedy is not that young people are willing to work hard.

It is that too many are still being handed outdated maps by institutions that confuse tradition with relevance.

A nation that trains its children for disappearing jobs is manufacturing future anxiety at scale.

The winners will not be the students with the neatest résumés. They will be the ones who combine education with optionality, practical leverage, and the courage to pivot when reality refuses to honor the plan.

Chapter 9

Relationship Capital

Who Trusts You is Everything in an AI World

Early in my career, I worked like a hired gun.

If a company needed fast results, measurable progress, and somebody willing to attack a problem without excuses, I was that person.

I loved it.

I loved the speed.

I loved the challenge.

I loved the recognition that came from being the one people called when something had to get fixed now.

The money was good.

The ego boost was even better.

There is a certain rush that comes from being known as the person who can walk into chaos and leave with results.

But over time, I realized something uncomfortable.

Results alone can make you valuable.

Relationships make you unforgettable.

That lesson changed everything.

I began studying how influence really worked inside companies.

Not the org chart.

Not the polished leadership slogans framed on conference room walls.

The real flow of trust.

Who actually spoke into decisions?

Who had the ear of leadership?

Who people believed when pressure was high.

Who got called into the room before opportunities became public?

That is when I learned one of the most important truths of my career:

It is not just what you know.

It is who knows what you are capable of.

In the old economy, skill could carry you far.

In the AI economy, visible trust may matter even more.

Why?

Because technical skill is becoming easier to imitate.

AI can now help millions of people write better emails, generate decent reports, build presentations, create code, and automate routine thinking tasks.

That means competence is becoming more common.

Common competence lowers market value.

Trust does the opposite.

Trust is built through consistency.

Through discretion.

Through pressure-tested execution.

Through how you handle setbacks.

Through how you make other people feel when the stakes are high.

AI can produce answers.

It cannot build human confidence in your judgment the way repeated shared wins can.

This is where many workers make a dangerous mistake.

They spend all their energy becoming more technically efficient while ignoring relationship equity.

They become productive but invisible.

Useful but disconnected.

Skilled but easy to replace.

The people who rise in the next decade will understand that trust is a force multiplier.

A recommendation from the right person can collapse years of struggle.

An introduction can create income faster than another certification.

A trusted reputation can protect you when departments shrink and budgets tighten.

People save people they trust.

That is the uncomfortable truth.

When companies reduce teams, the spreadsheet does not tell the whole story.

Leaders quietly ask:

Who do we trust with clients?

Who can handle complexity?

Who calms the room?

Who protects relationships that generate revenue?

Who has judgment when the software output is wrong?

This is where human advantage still lives.

I learned this personally when I stopped seeing work as a scoreboard and started seeing it as long-term trust building.

The real breakthrough in my career did not come from being the smartest person in the room.

It came from becoming the most dependable person in the network.

I invested time in relationships before I needed them.

Lunches mattered.

Conversations mattered.

Following through mattered.

Being the same person in success and pressure mattered.

Over time, doors opened that skill alone never would have unlocked.

This is how you beat AI.

You become trusted in ways software cannot replicate.

You build a reputation that survives market shifts.

You become the person whose name enters rooms before you do.

For students, this means mentors.

For workers, this means internal champions.

For entrepreneurs, this means distribution partners, referral networks, and customer trust.

For families, this means teaching children that reputation may become more valuable than raw credentials.

The American Dream in the AI era will increasingly belong to the people who combine technical leverage with human trust.

Anyone can access tools.

Not everyone can build belief.

And belief still moves opportunity faster than intelligence alone.

Example: The Manager Who Used Relationships to Become the AI Translator

Mark had spent twelve years as an operations manager for a regional distribution company.

He was respected, but not because he was the most technical person in the building.

He was respected because people trusted him.

Warehouse supervisors knew he listened before making decisions.

Drivers trusted that he understood real-world constraints.

The CFO trusted his numbers because he never exaggerated.

The CEO trusted him because when problems surfaced, Mark brought solutions instead of excuses.

Then the company deployed a new AI logistics platform.

The software could predict route efficiency, labor needs, maintenance schedules, and delivery bottlenecks far faster than any human team.

Within weeks, panic spread through middle management.

Many managers quietly feared they were being replaced.

Some resisted the software.

Some ignored it.

Some complained that leadership was "moving too fast."

Mark took a different path.

Because he had strong relationships across the company, he was invited into conversations others never even knew were happening.

Leadership asked him a simple question:

"Can this system actually work in the real world?"

That question changed his career.

Mark sat down with warehouse leads, dispatch teams, drivers, and finance.

He used AI to generate optimization models and labor forecasts, but then he did something the software could not do.

He translated those outputs into human reality.

He knew which drivers hated certain urban routes.

He knew which warehouse team slowed down after 3 p.m.

He knew which clients cared more about consistency than pure speed.

He knew where the data was technically correct but operationally dangerous.

Because people trusted him, they told him what the system was missing.

Because leadership trusted him, they listened when he adjusted the AI recommendations.

Instead of being replaced by the software, Mark became the bridge between the software and the people.

Within a year, he was promoted to a newly created role overseeing AI-assisted operations strategy.

The managers who focused only on protecting their old tasks were left behind.

Mark used relationships to gain access.

Then he used AI to create leverage.

That combination made him more valuable than either skill or software alone.

This is the future.

The winners in the AI economy will often be the people who become translators between machine intelligence and human trust systems.

That role cannot be earned through tools alone.

It is built through years of credibility.

This is how you beat AI.

You become the person trusted to make AI useful in the real world.

Proximity Creates Opportunity - Why Young Workers Must Get in the Room

Students and young workers need to understand something early:

Your future often changes in the rooms you choose to enter.

In an AI world, where the first rung of the ladder is disappearing, proximity to people already ahead of you becomes one of the fastest ways to replace the lost career pipeline.

That means networking can no longer be treated like an optional business-school exercise.

It is survival preparation.

A student should actively look for ways to build relationships with people operating in the top levels of local business and industry.

That might mean:

- a local business owner
- a plant manager
- a staffing company executive
- a sales director
- a warehouse operations leader
- a hospital administrator
- a construction company owner
- a logistics supervisor

- a banker
- a commercial real estate professional
- a manufacturing executive

Anyone with real hiring authority, market visibility, or operational responsibility can become a source of future-changing insight.

These people see the labor market before the public sees it.

They know which jobs are shrinking.

They know which skills are suddenly in demand.

They know which departments are experimenting with AI.

They know where internships are being cut and where new opportunities are quietly emerging.

That intelligence is priceless for someone trying to get ahead.

Young workers need to stop assuming these relationships only happen in formal office settings.

Opportunity often begins in ordinary places.

The gym.

A Rotary breakfast.

A local Chamber of Commerce event.

A church leadership group.

A youth sports booster club.

A neighborhood coffee shop.

Even casual social environments, like a sports bar or local restaurant, where business leaders regularly gather.

The point is not random small talk.

The point is repeated exposure and authentic curiosity.

People further ahead in their careers often respond well to young people who ask thoughtful questions, show respect, and clearly want to learn.

A simple conversation can open doors:

"What changes are you seeing in your business because of AI?"

"What skills do you think young people are underestimating right now?"

"If you were starting over at 22, what would you focus on first?"

Those questions do more than create conversation.

They create memory.

The young worker who becomes known as serious, curious, and action-oriented often gets remembered when opportunities surface.

That is how relationship capital begins.

Not through manipulation.

Through intelligent proximity.

This is how you beat AI early in your career.

You shorten the distance between where you are and where the decision-makers already stand.

Because the closer you get to real operators, the earlier you see where the future is moving.

Example: The Call Center Manager Who Built His Exit Before He Needed It

David was a mid-level manager overseeing workforce operations for a national credit card call center network.

For years, his job was built around managing people, service levels, staffing models, escalation procedures, and customer satisfaction metrics across multiple regional sites.

He was good at it.

He knew how to calm supervisors when call volumes spiked.

He understood how staffing shortages in Phoenix affected overflow in Omaha.

He could read the numbers behind customer complaints before the weekly reports ever reached senior leadership.

But David was paying attention to something most of his peers ignored.

AI was quietly changing the economics of customer service.

The company had started deploying voice AI, automated fraud alerts, predictive call routing, and intelligent self-service systems.

At first, leadership described it as support technology.

David knew better.

He understood that support technology has a way of becoming replacement technology once the numbers prove the savings.

Instead of pretending his experience alone would protect him, David began building relationship capital with discipline.

He networked tirelessly.

He stayed close to former directors who had moved into banking operations.

He kept in regular contact with staffing-company executives who specialized in financial-services placements.

He built relationships with leaders in fraud operations, collections, digital customer success, and fintech support teams.

He attended regional banking conferences.

He accepted every lunch, coffee, and industry mixer invitation he could reasonably fit into his schedule.

Not because he was desperate.

Because he was strategic.

He understood something critical:

In a market being reshaped by AI, access moves faster than applications.

David also kept his résumé current.

Not once a year.

Constantly.

Every major win was documented.

Reduced average handle time by 14 percent.

Improved supervisor retention.

Led rollout of AI-assisted call triage.

Integrated predictive staffing models that saved overtime costs.

Created escalation workflows between human agents and automated fraud systems.

His LinkedIn profile reflected where the industry was heading, not where it had been.

He stopped describing himself as a "call center manager."

He positioned himself as a **customer operations and AI-transition leader in financial services**.

That language mattered.

When the company eventually consolidated three call centers into one AI-assisted service hub, David was not blindsided.

Within two weeks of the internal announcement, three people from his network had already reached out.

A staffing executive told him a regional bank needed someone to oversee AI-human fraud escalation teams.

A former colleague connected him with a fintech company building premium white-glove customer support.

Another contact introduced him to a growing payments company that needed an operations leader who understood both legacy service teams and AI workflow integration.

David landed interviews before most of his peers had even updated their résumés.

He was hired into a higher-paying role within sixty days.

The managers who stayed isolated were left competing in the open market against thousands of displaced service leaders.

David never had to panic.

His network had already become his pipeline.

This is what relationship capital looks like in an AI world.

It is not just about getting ahead.

It is about making sure disruption never leaves you without options.

This is how you beat AI.

You build trusted pathways to your next move before your current role begins to disappear.

Example: A Great Mentor Makes All Things Possible.

Michael had spent nearly fifteen years rising through the ranks of a national insurance company.

By the time he reached the executive level, he understood the business from every angle.

Claims flow.

Policy retention.

Agent relationships.

Customer-service breakdowns.

Renewal economics.

He knew where clients stayed loyal and where they quietly left.

Most importantly, he understood the emotional side of insurance.

People do not call their insurance company when life is going well.

They call when something has gone wrong.

A storm.

A car accident.

A damaged roof.

A burst pipe.

A family emergency.

Moments like that require trust, speed, and empathy.

Then the company introduced a new AI-driven customer-service software platform.

On paper, the rollout looked brilliant.

Lower labor costs.

Fewer service representatives.

Automated claims intake.

Digital policy changes.

AI-powered customer chat.

Leadership knew the system was clunky.

They knew the user experience was frustrating.

They knew customers would become irritated by long loops, poor handoffs, and generic responses.

But the finance team had already run the numbers.

The labor savings from reducing high-quality service staff would more than offset the expected customer attrition.

It was a spreadsheet victory.

And a relationship disaster.

Michael saw immediately what leadership was willing to tolerate.

The company was choosing efficiency over trust.

That decision became his opening.

For years, Michael had maintained a strong relationship with an executive vice president from a competing insurance firm.

Some people would have viewed that relationship as dangerous.

Michael viewed it as educational.

The EVP had spent decades building agencies, leading regional growth, and understanding how trust drives long-term retention.

He had become more than an industry contact.

He was a mentor.

When Michael described what his company was doing, the mentor immediately saw the opportunity.

He told Michael something that changed the course of his life:

"If they are willing to abandon service, someone else will win by rebuilding it."

That sentence became the seed of a company.

Michael left and launched his own independent insurance agency.

From day one, he built the business around the exact weakness his former employer had knowingly created.

He hired the best customer-service representatives he could find.

Not the cheapest.

The best.

People who understood empathy.

People who followed through.

People who answered the phone like the customer actually mattered.

People who could combine technology with human reassurance.

His mentor was involved from the start.

He opened doors.

He shared carrier relationships.

He advised on hiring.

He helped shape compensation structures.

He warned Michael about common agency-growth mistakes.

He offered strategic guidance on which markets would be most vulnerable to customer frustration from poor AI deployments.

Every relationship Michael had built over the years now became fuel.

The results came fast.

Customers who left his former company because of the frustrating software experience began moving their policies to Michael's agency.

Not because his technology was radically better.

Because his **service experience was radically more human**.

He used AI, which improved speed and accuracy.

But he refused to let software become a wall between the customer and confidence.

Within three years, his agency was outperforming legacy retention expectations.

The irony was impossible to miss.

The very cost-cutting AI strategy designed to improve margins at his former employer had created the opening for Michael's growth.

This is the power of relationship capital in an AI world.

His mentor gave him more than advice.

He gave him perspective.

Pattern recognition.

Resources.

Confidence.

And speed.

This is how you beat AI.

You use trusted relationships to identify where technology creates pain, then build a better human-centered solution faster than the market.

The future belongs to the people who can see where efficiency has gone too far and rebuild trust where others abandoned it.

Chapter 10

Build the New Ladder Before Everyone Else Sees It

For generations, Americans were taught to climb.

Go to school.

Get the internship.

Take the entry-level role.

Work your way up.

The ladder was never perfect, but it existed.

Today, the bottom rungs are being cut off in real time.

Internships are shrinking. Junior analyst roles are being absorbed by software. Customer service teams are thinner. Administrative departments are disappearing behind automation layers that executives call "efficiency."

The old ladder is not broken.

It is being replaced.

The workers who thrive in the next decade will be the ones who understand a brutal truth early:

You may need to build your own first rung.

That means the new apprenticeship is no longer waiting for a company to train you.

It is:

- building a **proof portfolio**
- Freelancing for small projects
- using AI tools to create faster output
- networking into live problems
- Solving business pain before someone hires you
- learning to generate income before credentials are finished

The future belongs to people who can **demonstrate value before permission is granted**.

A college sophomore who builds three AI-assisted workflow case studies for local businesses may now be more employable than a graduate with no visible proof of execution.

A tradesman who learns predictive maintenance dashboards may outpace ten workers with more years but less adaptation.

A young worker who helps a local plant manager automate reporting on nights and weekends is already climbing the new ladder.

The ladder is still there.

It just no longer belongs to institutions.

It belongs to the builders.

This is where the 777-day rule becomes survival doctrine.

The first 777 days after you recognize disruption are where the gap is widest between what the market sees and what is actually coming.

Families that use those days to:

- stack skills
- build relationships
- create proof
- earn side income
- learn AI leverage
- study local labor shortages
- attach themselves to growing industries

It will create a separation that becomes almost impossible for others to catch.

The middle class will not be saved by waiting for schools, corporations, or government systems to rebuild the ladder.

It will be rebuilt by families, workers, and business owners who move first.

The American Dream still rewards builders.

It always has.

The only difference now is this:

The new ladder must often be built by the person climbing it.

Pivot, College Junior

Today's college junior has entered the most deceptive stage of the modern economy.

On paper, this should be the launch phase.

By junior year, students are supposed to be polishing résumés, lining up internships, interviewing for rotational programs, and preparing for that final sprint into the workforce.

But the old protocol was built for an economy that no longer exists.

The dangerous lie many students still believe is that staying on the traditional academic track alone will be enough. Good grades still matter, but in a labor market shaped by AI, automation, and shrinking entry-level pipelines, grades without proof are becoming little more than expensive decorations.

The modern junior year protocol must change.

By this point, every serious student needs to be operating on **four tracks at once**.

First, they need **skills that show immediate market usefulness**.

This means practical exposure to the tools already changing work:

- AI workflow tools
- prompt writing for research and analysis
- spreadsheet automation
- dashboard reporting
- CRM and customer service systems
- project management platforms
- data visualization
- process documentation
- digital communication systems

The goal is not mastery of every tool.

The goal is to prove they can step into a company and create value in the first thirty days.

Second, they need to build **relationships far beyond the campus bubble**.

This is where too many students lose momentum.

The smart junior is no longer only networking with professors and classmates. They are intentionally building real-world relationships with:

- business owners
- plant managers
- operations leaders
- staffing company executives
- logistics supervisors
- insurance managers
- local bankers
- hospital administrators
- trade company owners
- city leaders
- Anyone already responsible for hiring, workflow, budgets, or labor shortages.

The gym, the coffee shop, local Rotary lunches, alumni events, church groups, chamber meetings, trade expos, and even neighborhood business mixers all become career accelerators.

Opportunity now moves through trust before it moves through résumés.

Third, they must build a **visible proof portfolio**.

The new internship is often the portfolio.

A junior who can show:

- Three workflow optimization case studies
- an AI-assisted reporting project
- a redesigned customer service process
- a market research brief
- a predictive staffing dashboard
- a supply chain efficiency mockup
- a local business process improvement proposal

Has already separated from the crowd.

This portfolio proves the student is not waiting to be taught how to solve problems.

They are already solving them.

Finally, they need the **determination to survive a tricky economy without losing momentum**.

This may be the most important shift of all.

The new economy rewards students who can absorb rejection, adapt faster, and keep moving while their peers freeze.

Internships may disappear.

Entry-level roles may be delayed.

Companies may freeze hiring.

The winning junior keeps building anyway.

They freelance.

They volunteer for live business projects.

They solve problems for small local companies.

They shadow decision-makers.

They keep their LinkedIn current.

They refine their portfolio every month.

They learn how industries are quietly changing before the job descriptions catch up.

This is what it means to hit the road running now.

Not just with a degree.

But with **skills, relationships, proof, and grit already in motion**.

The students who follow this new protocol will not enter the workforce asking for an opportunity.

They will arrive already carrying it.

And in this economy, that difference changes everything.

Adult Ladders - Rebuilding Mid-Career Without Starting Over

The cruelest myth in the AI economy is that reinvention belongs only to the young.

It doesn’t.

In fact, mid-career adults may have the strongest foundation to climb the new ladder, because they already possess the one thing younger workers are still trying to earn: **Context.**

They understand customers.

They know how decisions get made.

They have seen budgets, politics, workflow failures, and the human cost of bad leadership.

They know where the bottlenecks live because they have spent years working around them.

That experience is not obsolete.

It is the raw material for the next ladder.

The protocol for adults is different from that of college juniors.

They are not building from zero.

They are converting experience into leverage.

The first move is to identify which parts of their current role are becoming **software tasks** and which parts remain **human leverage**.

A credit card call center manager may realize that scheduling, QA scoring, and first-level escalations are becoming automated.

But vendor relationships, executive communication, regulatory judgment, customer recovery strategy, and team morale remain deeply human.

That is the new rung.

The second move is to **attach AI to the existing authority**.

The winning adult worker does not fight the tools.

They use them to expand the scope of what they already know.

The insurance executive who learns AI-driven churn analysis becomes more valuable.

The plant supervisor who layers predictive maintenance dashboards onto years of floor knowledge becomes indispensable.

The logistics director who automates route reporting while deepening shipper relationships becomes harder to replace, not easier.

Adults must stop thinking in terms of job titles and start thinking in terms of **portable economic value**.

Ask:

- What business pain do I understand better than most people?
- What relationships have I built over ten or twenty years?
- What decisions do leaders trust me to influence?
- Where can AI make my judgment faster instead of replacing it?
- If this company vanished tomorrow, what value could I bring elsewhere by Monday?

That last question is the adult ladder test.

Because the new ladder is not a promotion.

It is **mobility.**

The strongest adult workers in the next decade will keep:

- Their résumé is permanently current
- a live portfolio of wins and metrics
- executive relationships inside and outside the company

- industry mentor connections
- speaking credibility
- visible proof of process improvements
- fluency with the AI systems reshaping their department

For many adults, the new ladder may even move outside employment entirely.

A customer service executive may launch a boutique service firm after watching a larger company destroy CX with automation. A plant leader may become an operations consultant. A banking manager may move into fraud and AI risk oversight. A trades veteran may build a local training academy around AI-assisted diagnostics.

This is not starting over.

This is **climbing sideways before climbing higher**.

That is how adults preserve income, dignity, and family momentum in a tricky economy.

The American Dream for adults in this era belongs to the people willing to rebuild the ladder while standing on it.

Chapter 11

The New Superstars - Trades Will Dominate the AI Economy

For years, America pushed one message with almost religious certainty:

Go to college.

Get the office job.

Work in air conditioning.

Stay clean.

Avoid manual labor.

An entire generation was taught to look at the trades as a backup plan.

That lie is now colliding headfirst with reality.

As artificial intelligence rapidly absorbs administrative work, customer service, scheduling, reporting, junior coding, bookkeeping, and many layers of entry-level analysis, the country is being forced to rediscover something it should never have forgotten:

The people who build, repair, install, power, and maintain the physical world are becoming the superstars of the next economy.

The future still needs humans.

Not just any humans.

It needs the men and women who can walk into a machine room, a manufacturing floor, a job site, a power station, a hospital mechanical system, a data center, or a robotics facility and make the real world function.

AI can recommend.

AI can monitor.

AI can predict.

But AI cannot physically replace a transformer in a storm, diagnose a failed compressor inside a hospital cooling system, repair a robotic weld arm on a midnight shift, or rebuild a control panel after a power surge destroys production.

That still takes skilled hands, trained judgment, and calm decision-making under pressure.

The trades are no longer the alternative path.

They are becoming the **front line of economic security**.

Why AI Makes the Trades More Valuable, Not Less

Most people misunderstand the relationship between AI and skilled labor.

They imagine AI replacing trades the same way it replaces office workers.

The opposite is more likely.

AI increases the value of trades because every intelligent system still depends on physical infrastructure.

Every AI server requires:

- electricians

- HVAC specialists
- data center cooling technicians
- fiber installation crews
- controls experts
- backup power specialists
- welders and steel fabricators
- industrial maintenance technicians

Every robotic factory requires:

- industrial electricians
- automation mechanics
- PLC programmers
- hydraulic and pneumatic specialists
- conveyor technicians
- machine alignment experts
- instrumentation specialists

Every smart building requires:

- controls technicians
- HVAC integration specialists
- access control installers
- network cabling teams
- low-voltage experts
- energy management professionals

In other words, **AI expands the number of physical systems that must be built and maintained by humans**.

The smarter the systems get, the more valuable the people become who understand both the physical equipment and the software layer guiding it.

That worker becomes nearly irreplaceable.

This is where the next American superstars are being built.

The Rise of the Hybrid Trade Professional

The winners in the trades will not just know the wrench.

They will know the screen.

The future belongs to the **hybrid trade professional**:

- The electrician who understands smart load balancing
- The HVAC expert who reads AI-driven building diagnostics
- The diesel mechanic who uses predictive maintenance dashboards
- The plant technician who works alongside robotics
- The welder who helps fabricate infrastructure for automation systems
- The lineman who supports smart grid technology
- The field service tech who uses AI fault detection before arriving on-site

This is how you beat AI.

You do not compete with it in pure software.

You become the human who uses AI to move faster in the physical world.

The person who can combine:

- human judgment
- field experience
- customer trust
- physical execution
- AI-assisted diagnostics

Will become one of the highest-value workers in America.

Why This Matters for the American Dream

The trades are also one of the last great ladders into the middle and upper middle class without traditional college debt.

That matters.

Families trying to preserve the American Dream need paths that still produce:

- strong income
- dignity
- skill ownership
- entrepreneurship
- local reputation
- long-term resilience
- The trades offer all of it.

A skilled HVAC owner.

A master electrician.

A welding contractor.

A specialty mechanic.

A robotics maintenance consultant.

A commercial plumbing company owner.

These are no longer "blue-collar" stereotypes.

These are **AI-era wealth builders**.

Many will outperform white-collar salaries that once looked safer.

The people who once mocked hard hats may soon be asking those same workers for jobs.

Again, irony. Humanity's most consistent renewable resource.

Patriotic Duty and the Next Generation

This chapter also carries a responsibility.

Older tradesmen, plant managers, foremen, and field leaders need to step forward and mentor the next generation.

America cannot preserve its industrial strength if knowledge dies at retirement.

It is a patriotic duty to teach:

- apprentices
- high school students
- displaced office workers
- veterans transitioning into civilian careers

- Young adults searching for real opportunity

The next generation must understand this truth:

The future is not only built by coders.

It is built by the people who make the physical world work.

The AI economy will not survive without them.

The American Dream will not survive without them.

And the families who recognize this early will position their children for one of the most stable, respected, and financially powerful career paths of the next twenty years.

The next superstars will not always wear suits.

Many of them will wear work boots.

And they may very well become the most valuable people in the future workplace.

From Apprentice to Master Across America's Skilled Trades

One of the greatest myths ever sold to young Americans was that the trades offered "just enough" to get by.

That may have been true for the unskilled laborer.

It is absolutely false for the licensed, specialized, and master-level trades professional.

The future belongs to skill holders.

As AI continues to compress white-collar middle management, the trades are quietly building a new class of six-figure earners, especially those who move from apprentice to journeyman to master, then eventually into ownership.

The ladder is clear.

Learn the craft.

Earn the license.

Master the specialty.

Own the relationships.

Then own the company.

That is one of the fastest remaining paths to wealth in America.

Recent 2026 salary guides show that licensed trades continue climbing sharply, with master-level specialists and owners routinely breaking six figures.

Electrical Trades

- **Apprentice Electrician:** $55,000-$75,000
- **Journeyman Electrician:** $75,000-$140,000
- **Master Electrician:** $140,000-$160,000+
- **Industrial / Data Center / EV Specialists:** $175,000+ in top markets

This is where AI infrastructure gets physically built. Data centers, smart buildings, EV charging, battery storage, and grid modernization all push electricity prices upward.

Plumbing / Pipefitting / Steamfitting

- **Apprentice:** $65,000-$85,000
- **Journeyman:** $85,000-$110,000
- **Master Plumber / Pipefitter:** $125,000-$140,000+

- **Industrial Steam / Process Systems:** $150,000+ with shutdown overtime

Hospitals, chip plants, pharmaceutical production, and AI-cooled facilities all depend on advanced piping systems. Humans still make those systems run.

HVAC / Refrigeration / Controls

- **Apprentice HVAC Tech:** $55,000-$70,000
- **Journeyman HVAC Tech:** $70,000-$90,000
- **Master HVAC / Controls Specialist:** $90,000-$130,000+
- **Critical Cooling / Data Center Specialists:** $150,000+

The hotter AI runs, the more valuable cooling experts become. Server farms don't survive on wishful thinking and startup buzzwords. They survive on compressors, airflow, and people who understand thermal load.

Welding / Fabrication / Ironwork

- **Apprentice Welder:** $52,000-$72,000
- **Journeyman Welder:** $72,000-$95,000
- **Master / Specialized Welder:** $80,000-$120,000+
- **Pipeline / Aerospace / Underwater:** $150,000+

The infrastructure of robotics, industrial automation, and energy expansion still begins with steel and the people who shape it.

Heavy Equipment / Diesel / Industrial Mechanics

- **Apprentice Diesel Tech:** $55,000-$70,000
- **Journeyman Mechanic:** $70,000-$95,000

- **Master Fleet / Industrial Mechanic:** $85,000-$120,000+
- **Mining / Rail / Energy / Field Service:** $140,000+

Machines still break. In fact, more automation means more machines that break in more expensive ways.

That is job security disguised as grease.

Power Linemen / Grid Technicians

- **Apprentice Lineworker:** $55,000-$65,000
- **Journeyman Lineman:** $80,000-$110,000
- **Master / Storm Response / Grid Specialist:** $130,000-$180,000+

One hurricane, one ice storm, one regional outage, and suddenly the most important person in America is wearing spikes and climbing gear. Grid modernization and AI energy demand make this one of the best long-term ladders in the country.

Carpentry / Finish / Commercial Construction

- **Apprentice Carpenter:** $50,000-$65,000
- **Journeyman Carpenter:** $65,000-$90,000
- **Master Finish / Commercial Lead:** $85,000-$115,000+
- **GC / Specialty Contractor Owner:** $150,000+

The real money here is mastery plus ownership, because eventually your hands train crews while your relationships build backlog.

Arborists / Tree Trimmers / Utility Clearing

- **Apprentice Tree Trimmer:** $50,000-$65,000
- **Journeyman Arborist / Climber:** $75,000-$95,000
- **Master Arborist / Utility Clearing Lead:** $85,000-$110,000+
- **Storm / Emergency Response Owner:** $150,000+

This one is underrated. As power grids expand and climate events intensify, skilled tree crews protecting utility corridors become essential infrastructure players.

The Real Wealth Move: Ownership

The master license is not the ceiling.

It is the doorway.

The electrician who starts a 5-van service company.

The HVAC master who builds a regional commercial maintenance firm.

The master plumber who specializes in medical facilities.

The arborist who lands utility contracts.

The welder who services industrial shutdowns.

These are the people who build real wealth.

Many trade business owners are clear:

- **$250,000-$500,000 annually**
- larger firms: **$1M+**
- enterprise regional firms: far beyond that

That is why the trades are no longer merely careers.

They are **wealth platforms for families who move early in the AI era**.

Trades, the superstars of the AI Era:

From Signing the Back of the Paycheck to Signing the Front - Why the Trades Are America's Fastest Path to Ownership

Here may be no better wealth ladder left in America than the skilled trades.

Think about what most people are told to do.

Spend four years in college.

Take on debt.

Fight for an entry-level office job.

Hope AI doesn't erase the role in thirty-six months.

Wait ten years for middle management.

Maybe someday earn enough to invest.

The trades flip that script.

A skilled tradesman can move from employee to owner faster than almost any other profession because the startup costs are low, the market demand is immediate, and the customer's need never disappears.

A licensed electrician does not need a glass tower office.

He needs:

- a truck or service van
- tools he often already owns

- insurance
- licensing
- a simple scheduling app
- a phone number
- relationships
- the courage to bet on himself

That is it.

The same is true for:

- plumbers
- HVAC technicians
- welders
- arborists
- tree crews
- diesel mechanics
- commercial cleaning specialists
- industrial maintenance contractors
- controls technicians
- linemen who move into utility subcontracting
- low-voltage and security installers
- refrigeration specialists
- Appliance Repair Pros
- elevator and escalator service experts

- roofing and gutter specialists
- smart-home / building automation installers

The barrier to ownership is shockingly low compared to almost every white-collar path.

No investors.

No app build.

No venture capital pitch deck.

No Silicon Valley costume party.

Just skill, reputation, and demand.

Instant Demand Creates Instant Revenue

This is what makes the trades uniquely attractive in the AI economy:

The work already exists before the company is formed.

That is rare.

Most businesses fail because they build first and hope customers appear later.

Trades businesses often launch with customers already waiting.

The new business owner may already have:

- past clients who trust his work
- vendors willing to refer him
- Former coworkers are feeding overflow jobs
- general contractors who need reliable help
- Plant managers are desperate for fast service

- homeowners asking for side work
- utility firms short on crews
- hospitals and data centers needing emergency specialists
- Property managers are begging for dependable vendors

The demand is not theoretical.

It is immediate.

A master HVAC technician can leave on Friday and have paying work by Monday.

A journeyman electrician with strong relationships can fill a week's schedule before the business cards arrive.

A tree trimmer with storm-season contacts may have more work than he can physically handle in the first month.

That is why this path is so powerful.

You are not creating demand.

You are stepping into unmet demand that already exists.

The AI Economy Makes Local Service More Valuable

Here is the deeper reason this chapter matters.

As AI removes layers of office labor, local skilled service becomes even more valuable because it is:

- immediate
- physical
- trust-based
- local

- reputation-driven
- hard to outsource
- impossible to offshore
- resistant to automation

A homeowner cannot upload a broken breaker panel to the cloud.

A hospital cannot ask a chatbot to physically restore chilled water to an ICU wing.

A manufacturing plant losing production at 2:00 a.m. does not care about your résumé format.

They care who answers the phone and shows up.

This is why local trade ownership may become one of the most recession-resistant business models of the next twenty years.

The One-Truck Empire

Every major service company begins with a single truck.

One truck.

One customer.

One referral.

One job done better than expected.

Then the flywheel starts.

One customer becomes five.

Five becomes twenty.

Twenty becomes a route.

A route becomes technicians.

Technicians become territory.

Territory becomes acquisition value.

This is not a theory.

This is how some of the largest home-service, commercial mechanical, industrial maintenance, and utility-support firms in America were built.

A single skilled worker becomes:

- technician
- estimator
- relationship builder
- recruiter
- trainer
- operations leader
- owner

And eventually, if done right, the seller.

The American Dream still lives here.

Not in the illusion of safety.

In ownership.

Why This Is So Attractive for the Next Generation

Young people need to understand what makes this path extraordinary.

A skilled trade is not merely employment.

It is a **license to print money**.

It offers:

- immediate earning power
- low debt
- fast skill progression
- rapid ownership path
- real local respect
- family wealth creation
- acquisition potential
- a sellable company
- generational handoff

No other major career path allows someone to build income, equity, and ownership this quickly with such low startup friction.

This is how families protect themselves in the AI era.

This is how communities rebuild the middle class.

This is how workers stop waiting for permission.

And no other industry offers the opportunity to go from **signing the back of their paycheck to signing the front** faster than the trades.

The future superstars of America may not sit behind desks.

They may own fleets.

They may own routes.

They may own service territories.

They may own regional companies.

And they may build wealth faster than the office workers who once looked down on them.

A beautiful little reversal, really. Civilization runs on competence, and eventually the market remembers.

The Best Jobs for Americans in the Next 5 Years to Beat AI and Protect the American Dream

If American workers want to stay ahead of AI over the next five years, they need to stop thinking like the last generation.

The old strategy was simple: get a degree, get an office job, learn the software, and climb the ladder.

That strategy is weakening fast.

AI is now most dangerous to work that is repetitive, screen-based, rules-based, report-driven, easy to monitor, easy to template, and easy to automate. That includes a growing share of administrative work, entry-level analysis, routine customer service, basic content production, scheduling, and many support functions that once looked safe.

The best jobs in the next five years will come from a different formula:

Physical skill, human trust, licensing, real-world problem solving, technical depth, regulation, and the ability to work alongside AI instead of against it.

That is the dividing line.

The workers who win will not be the ones trying to outrun software at its own game. They will be the ones doing work that combines judgment, accountability, physical execution, relationships, and consequence.

Here is where that **future is strongest**.

1. Nurse Practitioners and Advanced Practice Nursing

This is one of the clearest examples of work AI will assist but not replace. Patients still want human judgment, real accountability, bedside trust, and licensed medical decision-making. BLS projects employment for nurse practitioners, nurse anesthetists, and nurse midwives to grow **35% from 2024 to 2034**, and reports a **median annual wage of $132,050** in May 2024.

Why it survives AI: medicine is high-trust, high-liability, emotionally human, and heavily regulated. Software can help with documentation, triage, and diagnostics, but a machine is not the person families want delivering care decisions when the stakes are real.

2. Physician Assistants

Physician assistants sit in another strong AI-resistant lane: licensed, hands-on, patient-facing, and clinically accountable. BLS says physician assistants had a **median annual wage of $133,260** in May 2024, with employment projected to grow **20% from 2024 to 2034**.

Why it survives AI: the job blends medical reasoning, patient interaction, legal accountability, and team-based care. AI can support the workflow, but it does not absorb the responsibility. Humans still get blamed, sued, trusted, and relied upon. Funny how that part never gets outsourced.

3. Registered Nurses

Registered nursing remains one of the strongest broad-based career paths in America because it offers scale, portability, and constant demand. BLS reports a **median annual wage of $93,600** and projects **189,100 openings per year on average** over the decade, with employment growing **5% from 2024 to 2034**.

Why it survives AI: Nurses do far more than process information. They observe, reassure, escalate, teach, adapt, and make judgment calls in real time around actual human beings. AI helps nurses. It does not eliminate the need for them.

4. Dental Hygienists

Dental hygiene is a good example of a practical, licensed, human-facing role that pays well without requiring the longest educational runway. BLS lists a **median annual wage of $94,260** and projects **7% employment growth** from 2024 to 2034.

Why it survives AI: the work is clinical, hands-on, local, and trust-based. A chatbot is not cleaning teeth, monitoring gum health, or reading a nervous patient in a chair. At least not until society gets much weirder than it already is.

5. Occupational Therapists and Physical Therapists

These jobs sit in a valuable category: they blend medical knowledge, human motivation, rehabilitation planning, and physical observation. BLS reports a **median annual wage of $98,340** for occupational therapists with **14% projected growth**, and a **median annual wage of $101,020** for physical therapists with **11% projected growth** from 2024 to 2034.

Why they survive AI: recovery is not just technical. It is behavioral, personal, emotional, and adaptive. Progress depends on reading people, coaching them, and adjusting treatment in the real world. Machines can recommend. Humans still have to move the person forward.

6. Electricians

Electricians are one of the strongest non-college or apprenticeship-first paths because the entire AI economy still depends on physical power, controls, buildings, backup systems, charging networks, and infrastructure. BLS lists a **median annual wage of $82,350, 9% projected growth** from 2024 to 2034, and about **81,000 openings per year**.

Why it survives AI: every "smart" system still runs through dumb reality: wire, power, load, failure, weather, code, safety, installation, and repair. AI increases demand for electrical work because more intelligence means more infrastructure.

7. Electrical Power-Line Installers and Repairers

This is one of the most underrated careers in the country. BLS reports a **median annual wage of $92,560** and **7% projected growth** from 2024 to 2034, with about **10,700 openings per year**.

Why it survives AI: the grid still has to be built, repaired, restored, and hardened. Data centers, electrification, severe weather, and rising power demand all increase the importance of this work. The people who keep the lights on do not get replaced by PowerPoint.

8. Elevator and Escalator Installers and Repairers

This is one of the best-paid skilled trades in America. BLS puts the **median annual wage at $106,580** with **5% projected growth** from 2024 to 2034.

Why it survives AI: these are complicated, regulated systems tied to physical buildings, safety standards, and emergency service needs. The work is technical, licensed, local, and high-consequence. Exactly the sort of thing AI helps schedule but does not physically solve.

9. Industrial Machinery Mechanics and Millwrights

As more factories automate, the need for skilled humans who maintain and repair that automation rises with it. BLS reports a **median annual wage of $73,510** for industrial machinery mechanics, machinery maintenance workers, and millwrights, with overall employment projected to grow **15% from 2024 to 2034**.

Why it survives AI: robots, conveyor systems, packaging lines, sensors, motors, and production equipment all need human troubleshooting when they fail. More automation means more systems to maintain, not fewer breakdowns. Machines are wonderful right up until they jam at 2:11 a.m.

10. Wind Turbine Technicians

This is a smaller occupation, but one of the fastest-growing in the country. BLS reports a **median annual wage of $72,580** and projects **50% employment growth** from 2024 to 2034.

Why it survives AI: renewable energy still depends on field maintenance, climbing, diagnostics, repair, and real-world service work. This is another example of how the future rewards people who can work with advanced systems in physical environments.

11. Aircraft Mechanics and Avionics Technicians

Aviation is another field where safety, regulation, inspection, and specialized skills protect workers from rapid automation. BLS reports a **median annual wage of $78,680** for aircraft mechanics and service technicians and **$81,390** for avionics technicians in May 2024.

Why it survives AI: aircraft maintenance is compliance-heavy, safety-critical, and unforgiving. There is no appetite for casual mistakes when machines carrying human beings are involved. That tends to focus the mind.

12. Information Security Analysts

Not every strong path is physical. Cybersecurity is one of the better digital careers because the attack surface keeps growing, the stakes are high, and defenders need judgment, investigation, and response skills. BLS reports a **median annual wage of $124,910** for information security analysts in May 2024.

Why it survives AI: attackers use AI too. That means companies still need humans who can interpret threats, make risk decisions, investigate incidents, and understand business consequences. Cybersecurity is not just code. It is defense, trust, and response under pressure.

13. Data Scientists and Operations Research Analysts

These jobs are more exposed to AI than the hands-on fields, but they remain strong when paired with real business domain knowledge. BLS reports a **median annual wage of $112,590** for data scientists with **34% projected growth**, and a **median annual wage of $91,290** for operations research analysts with **21% projected growth** from 2024 to 2034.

Why they survive AI: the winning version of this career is not "person who makes charts." It is "a person who understands operations, economics, risk, decision-making, and how to turn data into action." Pure spreadsheet labor is vulnerable. Domain-based analytical leadership is not nearly as easy to replace.

14. Electrical Engineers and Technical Systems Engineers

Engineers who design, integrate, and troubleshoot real systems should remain in a strong position, especially around power, controls, semiconductors, defense, automation, and infrastructure. BLS reports a **median annual wage of $121,910** for electrical engineers in May 2024.

Why it survives AI: engineering with real-world consequences still requires design judgment, tradeoffs, testing, safety, and integration across messy physical systems. AI helps with simulation and drafting, but the engineer still owns the outcome.

15. Logisticians and Transportation/Distribution Managers

Supply chains got a brutal reminder in recent years that physical movement, planning, and contingency management matter. BLS reports a **median annual wage of $80,880** for logisticians with **17% projected growth**, and a **median annual wage of $102,010** for transportation, storage, and distribution managers.

Why they survive AI: software can optimize routes and inventory, but real-world logistics includes disruptions, exceptions, negotiation, vendor reliability, bottlenecks, and physical consequences. The best people in this field use AI. They do not get replaced by it.

16. Sales Engineers

This is one of the smartest "human edge" careers for people who can combine technical understanding with trust and persuasion. BLS reports a **median annual wage of $121,520** and **5% projected growth** from 2024 to 2034.

Why it survives AI: complex sales still require credibility, context, relationship management, timing, and the ability to guide buyers through risk. AI can help qualify leads and write follow-up emails, but it does not replace the closer who understands both the product and the customer's fear.

The Pattern Workers Should Notice

When you stand back from the list, the pattern is obvious.

The best jobs in the next five years are not random. They cluster around a few protective advantages:

1. **Licensed and regulated work.** If the job requires formal credentials, legal accountability, or compliance, AI adoption moves more slowly, and human oversight remains essential.
2. **Physical work in the real world.** If the job requires hand movement, site conditions, tools, repair, installation, or field service, it is much harder to automate fully.
3. **Human trust and care.** Healthcare, rehabilitation, and patient-facing roles remain strong because people still want reassurance, empathy, explanation, and responsibility from another human being.
4. **High-stakes technical judgment.** Cybersecurity, engineering, aviation maintenance, and advanced analytics survive when the worker is not just following rules but making consequential decisions.
5. **Ability to use AI as a tool.** The strongest workers will not reject AI. They will use it to move faster, document better, diagnose earlier, and make sharper decisions. That is the real competition. Not human versus machine, but human with machine versus human without it. That last group is going to have a rough time.

Bottom Line

If you are an American worker trying to choose a path for the next five years, stop chasing jobs that are easy to digitize, easy to monitor, easy to template, and easy to offshore.

Move toward work that is harder to fake.

Move toward work that demands trust.

Move toward work that touches the real world.

Move toward work that requires a license, a skill, a body, a reputation, or a consequence.

That is where the future still pays.

That is where AI becomes your tool instead of your replacement.

And for millions of Americans, that may be the difference between staying in the middle class and watching it disappear from the wrong side of a screen.

Chapter 12

The High Achiever AI Network

The workers and families who win in the next decade will not operate alone.

The speed of AI change is now too fast for isolated awareness.

One company rolls out call summarization.

Another automates first-round interviews.

A bank quietly cuts junior underwriting analysts.

A logistics company deploys route optimization and trims dispatch.

A hospital centralizes scheduling through AI-assisted intake.

By the time the public sees layoffs, the smart network has already seen the software purchase orders, the workflow changes, the reassigned tasks, and the shrinking meeting invites.

That is why the future belongs to **networks of high achievers who share early signals**.

The High Achiever AI Network should be built around one mission:

Spot labor disruption early enough for people to pivot before the market floods.

The members are not just "AI enthusiasts."

They are:

- plant managers
- operations leaders
- HR executives
- staffing owners
- recruiters
- insurance managers
- logistics directors
- trade business owners
- college juniors building portfolios
- mid-career adults protecting families
- founders testing AI inside workflows
- trusted local business leaders
- workers are already one layer ahead of disruption

The protocol is simple.

Every member contributes **field intelligence**.

Not rumors.

Not fear.

Not clickbait.

Real signals:

- new software vendors entering departments
- disappearing internships

- reduced overtime
- workflow consolidation
- tasks shifted from people to systems
- new AI reporting dashboards
- customer service bot deployments
- fraud monitoring changes
- QA scoring automation
- hiring freezes hidden behind "restructuring."
- shifts in local trade demand
- local plant or office technology upgrades

This becomes a **survival network for the middle class**.

How to start it in the real world:

1) Build the first 25-member circle

Start with people you already know:

- Rotary contacts
- local bankers
- plant managers
- staffing executives
- insurance leaders
- trades owners
- former corporate contacts
- college career center allies

- Your author audience

You don't need to scale first.

You need **signal quality**.

2) Create a monthly AI disruption briefing

Every member sends:

- what changed
- What software appeared
- What roles are thinning
- What new skills are suddenly valuable
- Which vendors are being tested
- where labor shortages still remain human-first

This becomes the intelligence layer.

3) Build a shared pivot board

Each signal must connect to:

- replacement risk
- new opportunities
- local shortages
- AI-adjacent roles
- consulting openings
- freelance work
- retraining paths

No one should leave with fear alone.

Every signal needs a **countermove**.

4) Create a trust code

No gossip.

No company secrets.

No panic.

No politics.

Only practical labor signals and career pivots.

The purpose is to help families move faster than disruption.

This network could eventually become:

- a paid mastermind
- a Substack intelligence community
- a private Telegram or Circle group
- a speaking event pipeline
- a chapter-ending workbook tool
- a branded extension of the book itself

The people nearing retirement are sitting on exactly what the younger workforce is starving for:

- pattern recognition
- industry memory
- relationship maps
- hard-earned judgment
- quiet warning signs

- Political navigation inside companies'
- vendor history
- , and client trust
- “I’ve seen this movie before” instincts.

If they walk out the door with that knowledge, the next generation starts blind.

This belongs directly after the network blueprint as an expansion section.

The Legacy Layer - Why the Final Years of a Career Matter Most

The Human Reliance Network cannot be built only on speed.

It must also be built on **wisdom**.

That means the men and women who are nearing retirement, or already standing at the final chapter of their careers, must recognize a new responsibility.

Their job is no longer only to protect their own legacy.

It is to **transfer their ladder to the next generation before the rung disappears**.

For decades, experienced professionals carried invisible maps inside their heads.

They know:

- Which skills survive every cycle
- How leadership really makes decisions
- How industries quietly consolidate

- What bad software rollouts look like before the press release
- Which vendors overpromise
- Which customers stay loyal
- How to recover trust after operational mistakes
- where margins really come from
- When management language signals hidden restructuring
- How to tell the difference between efficiency and the beginning of replacement

This intelligence cannot be allowed to retire.

The structure of the Human Reliance Network must therefore include a **Legacy Layer**.

This is a formal mentor and intelligence transfer system where senior professionals step into defined roles:

1) Industry Mentors

Retired executives, plant leaders, district managers, HR veterans, bankers, insurance leaders, logistics directors, and trades owners become assigned mentors to younger members.

Not motivational fluff.

Real field guidance:

- What roles are durable
- What signals to watch
- who to know
- how to survive office politics

- How to prepare for the sideways move before the layoff

2) Career Ladder Maps

Veterans help younger members understand the **hidden ladders** inside industries.

Not just titles.

Real ladders:

- Who influences promotions
- What metrics actually matter
- When to move companies
- when to stay
- where AI is compressing the lower rungs
- where human trust still expands opportunity

3) Relationship Bridges

The most valuable thing senior professionals possess is not knowledge.

It is access.

The Legacy Layer must allow retiring leaders to make:

- warm introductions
- board connections
- vendor referrals
- banker relationships
- plant tours
- executive lunches

- shadowing opportunities
- speaking introductions
- first client referrals
- regional industry access

One trusted introduction can save younger workers years.

4) Historical Pattern Intelligence

Older generations have seen recessions, mergers, ERP disasters, outsourcing waves, software failures, offshoring cycles, and management fads come and go.

That historical memory is priceless.

AI disruption feels new, but many of its **behavioral signals are old**:

- cost reduction language
- workflow centralization
- vendor dependency
- quiet headcount freezes
- restructuring by euphemism
- Morale collapsed before the announcement.

Veterans can teach younger workers how to read the tea leaves early.

5) The Patriotic Duty of Career Stewardship

This is bigger than career coaching.

For those at the end of their careers, this is a duty to the country itself.

Previous generations fought wars, built companies, protected institutions, and expanded the middle class.

Now the duty is to **pass the operating knowledge forward fast enough to preserve upward mobility for the next generation of American workers**.

The Human Reliance Network becomes strongest when experience does not retire.

It compounds.

That is how the ladder survives.

Not because institutions preserve it.

Because one generation deliberately hands it to the next.

Chapter 13

The Human Reliance Network

I am proposing that America begin building something new.

A Human Reliance Network.

A controlled-access achievement network where workers, students, families, executives, tradespeople, and entrepreneurs can plug into **all things AI jobs, career defense, and opportunity creation**.

This is not social media noise.

This is not another content feed.

This is not fear porn for clicks.

This is a **human-first operating system for surviving and winning in the AI economy**.

The idea is simple:

Anyone who joins gains controlled access to the tools, signals, relationships, and opportunities needed to stay ahead of labor disruption.

The Human Reliance Network would include every practical advantage humans need.

1) National AI Job Defense Board

A live job board focused on:

- AI-resilient careers
- AI-adjacent roles

- automation-proof trades
- management jobs requiring human judgment
- consulting roles
- workflow redesign jobs
- customer recovery roles
- trust and relationship-heavy positions
- fraud and compliance oversight
- AI supervision roles
- skilled trade expansions
- local business leadership opportunities

This becomes the **job radar system**.

2) Rapid Skill Training Library

A video vault and fast-action learning hub with:

- AI workflow training
- prompt engineering for business users
- spreadsheet automation
- reporting dashboards
- CRM mastery
- project management systems
- customer experience recovery
- trade diagnostics with AI overlays
- logistics and route optimization tools

- insurance and risk workflows
- sales enablement tools
- executive communication upgrades
- portfolio building tutorials
- resume modernization
- interview prep for AI-era roles

The goal is simple:

learn tonight, use tomorrow, monetize next week.

3) Human Contact Network

This may be the most powerful piece.

Members gain structured access to:

- recruiters
- staffing executives
- local plant managers
- business owners
- trades leaders
- mentors
- insurance executives
- logistics operators
- regional bankers
- startup founders
- University Career Allies

- private coaching groups
- alumni pathways
- speaking communities

Opportunity still moves through people.

The Human Reliance Network makes sure people are never isolated.

4) Early Warning AI Signals

A protected intelligence feed where members share:

- shrinking departments
- disappearing internships
- software rollouts
- workflow automation
- hidden hiring freezes
- vendor changes
- new executive mandates
- local industry shifts
- rising trade shortages
- regional economic pivots
- sectors hiring faster than expected

This becomes a **national disruption radar**.

5) Proof Portfolio Builder

Templates and systems for members to create:

- business case studies
- workflow redesign samples
- AI productivity demonstrations
- process improvement decks
- consulting proof packs
- customer recovery playbooks
- predictive dashboard mockups
- trade diagnostic reports
- Operational efficiency wins

The new résumé is proof.

This makes the proof systematic.

6) Family Resilience Protocol

A special section for households:

- teenager career planning
- college junior protocol
- adult ladder pivots
- spouse income diversification
- regional relocation maps
- emergency upskilling sprints
- Family Financial Resilience Checklists

- side business playbooks

This turns the household into a unit of strength.

7) Entrepreneur Launch Zone

For people forced out of roles or moving early:

- small business startup maps
- consulting frameworks
- speaking business models
- digital product ideas
- AI service business kits
- local service business modernization
- customer acquisition playbooks
- automation consulting offers
- licensing and franchise ideas

This is where disruption becomes ownership.

The Human Reliance Network would be the first place where workers do not merely react to AI.

They **coordinate against disruption and toward opportunity together**.

This is how humans beat speed:

through signal,

through trust,

through preparation,

through each other.

Intergenerational wisdom transfer.

The people nearing retirement are sitting on exactly what the younger workforce is starving for:

- pattern recognition
- industry memory
- relationship maps
- hard-earned judgment
- quiet warning signs
- Political navigation inside companies
- , vendor history
- , and client trust
- "I've seen this movie before" instincts.

If they walk out the door with that knowledge, the next generation starts blind.

This belongs directly after the network blueprint as an expansion section.

The Legacy Layer - Why the Final Years of a Career Matter Most

The Human Reliance Network cannot be built only on speed.

It must also be built on **wisdom**.

That means the men and women who are nearing retirement, or already standing at the final chapter of their careers, must recognize a new responsibility.

Their job is no longer only to protect their own legacy.

It is to **transfer their ladder to the next generation before the rung disappears**.

For decades, experienced professionals carried invisible maps inside their heads.

They know:

- Which skills survive every cycle
- How leadership really makes decisions
- How industries quietly consolidate
- What bad software rollouts look like before the press release
- Which vendors overpromise
- Which customers stay loyal
- How to recover trust after operational mistakes
- where margins really come from
- When management language signals hidden restructuring
- How to tell the difference between efficiency and the beginning of replacement

This intelligence cannot be allowed to retire.

The structure of the Human Reliance Network must therefore include a **Legacy Layer**.

This is a formal mentor and intelligence transfer system where senior professionals step into defined roles:

1) Industry Mentors

Retired executives, plant leaders, district managers, HR veterans, bankers, insurance leaders, logistics directors, and trades owners become assigned mentors to younger members.

Not motivational fluff.

Real field guidance:

- What roles are durable
- What signals to watch
- who to know
- how to survive office politics
- How to prepare for the sideways move before the layoff

2) Career Ladder Maps

Veterans help younger members understand the **hidden ladders** inside industries.

Not just titles.

Real ladders:

- Who influences promotions
- What metrics actually matter
- When to move companies
- when to stay
- where AI is compressing the lower rungs
- where human trust still expands opportunity

3) Relationship Bridges

The most valuable thing senior professionals possess is not knowledge.

It is access.

The Legacy Layer must allow retiring leaders to make:

- warm introductions
- board connections
- vendor referrals
- banker relationships
- plant tours
- executive lunches
- shadowing opportunities
- speaking introductions
- first client referrals
- regional industry access

One trusted introduction can save younger workers years.

4) Historical Pattern Intelligence

Older generations have seen recessions, mergers, ERP disasters, outsourcing waves, software failures, offshoring cycles, and management fads come and go.

That historical memory is priceless.

AI disruption feels new, but many of its **behavioral signals are old**:

- cost reduction language
- workflow centralization
- vendor dependency
- quiet headcount freezes
- restructuring by euphemism
- Morale collapsed before the announcement.

Veterans can teach younger workers how to read the tea leaves early.

5) The Patriotic Duty of Career Stewardship

This is bigger than career coaching.

For those at the end of their careers, this is a duty to the country itself.

Previous generations fought wars, built companies, protected institutions, and expanded the middle class.

Now the duty is to **pass the operating knowledge forward fast enough to preserve upward mobility for the next generation of American workers**.

The Human Reliance Network becomes strongest when experience does not retire.

It compounds.

That is how the ladder survives.

Not because institutions preserve it.

Because one generation deliberately hands it to the next.

Add to this that we need to come together and share, as it's our responsibility and patriotic duty to support and help the next generations have the ability to enjoy the American Dream.

The American Dream has always belonged to those working to catch it.

Now it also belongs to those willing to **pass the blueprint forward**.

Chapter 14

Rise Before The Door Closes

Most people do not lose their future in one dramatic moment.

They lose it in stages.

First comes the **Head-in-the-Sand Stage**.

This is the most dangerous phase because nothing appears broken yet. The paycheck still arrives. The title still sounds respectable. The routines still feel familiar. The degree on the wall still whispers the lie that credentials alone create safety.

But under the surface, the pipeline is already breaking.

The internship that used to lead to the first real job has been cut.

The junior analyst role is now half software.

The customer service floor is half empty.

The administrative ladder that once trained tomorrow's managers is gone.

The quiet layoffs started months before the formal layoff ever arrived.

This is where people destroy themselves with delay.

They mistake **temporary comfort for permanent relevance**.

That is why this book keeps returning to the same unforgiving truth:

The people who rise in the AI era will move while others are still explaining why they have time.

That is where your **777 Doctrine** becomes the reader's marching orders.

For the next **777 days**, the reader must treat reinvention like a mission, not a hobby.

Day 1 through Day 90

Research obsessively.

Study where AI is compressing roles.

Learn which industries still reward scarce human judgment, trust, physical execution, leadership, relationship leverage, and ownership.

Day 91 through Day 365

Skill stacking begins.

This is where they learn AI tools, sharpen communication, build trade-level competence, improve sales ability, understand systems, and develop a body of work that proves usefulness.

Day 366 through Day 777

Expansion.

Monetize the skill.

Turn the skill into consulting, side income, equity, partnerships, licensing, content, apprenticeship, trade mastery, or business ownership.

This is the stage where the worker stops being labor only and starts becoming leverage.

That transitions perfectly into your **Learn. Earn. Own. Repeat.** Framework.

This needs to be a permanent life loop.

Learn.

Acquire a skill the market is actively paying for now, not one that schools are still selling based on yesterday.

Earn.

Use that skill immediately in the real world. Freelance, intern, apprentice, trade, sell, consult, build. The market is the only honest teacher left.

Own.

This is the wealth move most workers miss.

Ownership is where labor becomes freedom.

A service route.

A small agency.

A local trade business.

A digital asset.

A training community.

A software workflow.

A content library.

A book series.

A customer list.

A portfolio of case studies.

A network.

Anything that pays after the hours are finished.

Repeat.

The cycle never ends because stability itself is dead.

The repeaters win.

Then hit the **broken pipeline** with more force.

College students need to understand that the old path is collapsing in real time.

The pipeline used to look simple:

degree → internship → entry role → promotion → middle class.

Now the first two rungs are cracking.

Internships are shrinking.

Entry-level white-collar jobs are disappearing.

Administrative proving grounds are being automated.

Junior coding work is being absorbed by AI copilots.

The "learn on the job" era is fading.

So students must choose a new path:

portfolio first, credentials second.

Everyone now needs a portfolio.

Not artists.

Not just coders.

Everyone.

A portfolio means proof.

Case studies.

Projects.

AI workflows.

Sales wins.

Marketing experiments.

Business plans.

Operational fixes.

Trade mastery photos.

Before-and-after outcomes.

Revenue impact.

A real system improved by your thinking.

A résumé tells people what you hope is true.

A portfolio proves what is already true.

This is where mentors become oxygen.

The fastest way to compress ten years into two is borrowed experience.

A mentor helps readers:

- avoid dead-end industries
- Spot the broken pipeline early
- build introductions
- borrow confidence
- shortcut political mistakes
- Find ownership paths faster

- understand where AI creates opportunity instead of fear

College students especially need this pressure.

Do not major in comfort.

Do not choose the path with the easiest emotional approval.

Choose the lane where scarcity, proof, relationships, and ownership still matter.

The student who combines:

- AI fluency
- communication
- mentorship
- proof-of-work portfolio
- ownership ambition

Will outrun peers who are still chasing titles.

And this is where you land the hardest wealth truth in the entire book:

The real wealth move is ownership.

Not wages alone.

Not promotions alone.

Not titles.

Ownership.

The people who will preserve the American Dream in the AI era will own:

- businesses
- trade routes
- client relationships
- platforms
- books
- media brands
- real estate
- intellectual property
- distribution
- Systems AI cannot be replaced because they are built on trust and control

That's the final pressure point.

Waiting is no longer neutral.

Waiting is an active decision to fall behind.

The reader must feel this:

If you are still in the Head-in-the-Sand Stage, the danger is not AI.

The danger is the story you keep telling yourself about why tomorrow is soon enough.

Rise now.

Build now.

Learn now.

Find mentors now.

Create proof now.

Move toward ownership now.

No one is coming to save you.

That means the future still belongs to the people willing to take it.

Epilogue:

What I Saw on the Road as America Entered the AI Era

Over the last three years, I spent time moving across the country, city by city, airport by airport, hotel lobby by hotel lobby, talking to people whose lives will either be reshaped by artificial intelligence or strengthened by how they respond to it.

At first, the concern barely existed.

People heard the letters A and I and treated them like another buzzword born in Silicon Valley, another shiny object for tech conferences and LinkedIn posts.

But I watched that change.

The shift was subtle in the beginning. Tech leaders spoke about AI with swagger, like proud architects unveiling the next great machine. Their language was bold, almost celebratory. Efficiency. Scale. Productivity. Transformation.

Then I watched the swagger change.

It went from a confident walk to a dead sprint.

The conversations became faster, sharper, and more urgent. The same leaders who once spoke about enhancement started quietly acknowledging replacement. First tasks. Then roles. Then departments. The entire occupation.

That was the moment I knew the AI era had truly begun.

What made it real was not the headlines.

It was the people.

I sat down with workers from completely different worlds, and despite the distance between their jobs, their fears sounded hauntingly similar.

The first was a **powerline worker**, a veteran lineman in Minnesota. We sat in a Denny's before sunrise, coffee thick enough to stand a spoon in, his hands scarred from decades of storms and emergency restorations.

He leaned back and said, *"They're bringing in drones, predictive sensors, grid intelligence. They're saying AI can spot failures before we even roll a truck. Makes me wonder how many trucks they'll need rolling in five years."*

He wasn't afraid of hard work disappearing.

He was afraid of the ladder changing beneath the younger workers.

I told him what this book keeps proving:

The physical danger, judgment, and real-world troubleshooting of restoring live power in chaos still belong to humans.

AI can predict.

It can map.

It can optimize dispatch.

But when an ice storm snaps three poles, and a transformer blows in the dark, people still need experienced hands and nerves.

The solution wasn't fear.

It was elevation.

The next generation of linemen must become **AI-assisted grid specialists**, the people who understand both field repair and the digital intelligence controlling modern infrastructure.

The trade doesn't disappear.

It becomes more elite.

The second interview happened in a hotel lobby in Dallas.

A **front desk clerk**, maybe late twenties, sharp, polished, the kind of professional who could calm an angry guest in thirty seconds flat.

She told me, *"The kiosk handles check-in now. The chatbot answers booking questions. Corporate keeps saying AI frees us up for higher-value work, but fewer people are being scheduled."* Hospitality front-desk roles are already being compressed as kiosks, booking chatbots, and AI concierge systems take over transactional tasks.

There it was again.

The broken pipeline.

The front desk used to be the first rung to management. Now the rung itself is vanishing. Industry reporting increasingly warns that entry-level hospitality roles are being removed before workers ever get a chance to climb.

I told her the answer was to stop identifying as "front desk."

She needed to become a **guest-experience revenue management talent**.

Learn upselling.

Learn event operations.

Learn customer retention systems.

Learn AI personalization tools.

Own the guest relationship, not the check-in process.

The future belongs to people who move from task ownership to outcome ownership.

The third conversation was one of the most revealing.

An **aircraft salesman** from Wichita, polished, confident, old-school relationship guy.

We met near an FBO lounge, watching jets taxi while he explained how AI is changing even luxury and high-ticket trust sales.

He said, *"Customers now come in with AI-generated comparisons, financing models, maintenance projections, and resale scenarios before I even shake their hand. Information used to be my edge."*

That line stayed with me.

Information is no longer the edge. Interpretation is. Trust is. Judgment is.

I told him his future is bigger than sales if he adapts.

He must become an **aviation acquisition advisor**.

AI can produce comparison sheets.

It cannot replace lived flight experience, mission-fit judgment, maintenance network trust, insurance pitfalls, hangar strategy, ownership tax structures, and the emotional confidence buyers need before signing a seven-figure check.

His job is safe only if he rises above being the keeper of facts and becomes the translator of consequences.

The fourth interview hit hardest on the human side.

A **Pennsylvania nurse practitioner**, with exhausted eyes and a compassionate voice, was sitting with me in a quiet café after a hospital shift.

She said, *"The charting software already feels like it watches us. They're talking about AI diagnostics, intake summaries, and follow-up automation. My fear isn't replacement. My fear is losing the human side under all the screens."*

That concern matters.

Healthcare may be one of the clearest examples of augmentation over replacement.

AI can summarize charts, flag anomalies, suggest pathways, and reduce documentation burden.

But patients do not trust algorithms.

They trust the nurse who notices fear in their face before the words come out.

I told her the future nurse becomes more valuable, not less, when AI removes clerical drag.

The nurse who combines bedside empathy with AI-supported decision tools becomes the highest-value clinician in the room.

The machine handles signal detection.

The human handles meaning.

And that is what I kept seeing across America.

The fear was never really about technology.

It was about **identity**.

People were asking the same silent question:

If the task I built my career around changes, who do I become next?

My answer never changed.

You rise.

You become the mentor.

You become the portfolio builder.

You become the ownership thinker.

You become the person who learns faster than the disruption spreads.

The AI era does not reward denial.

It rewards motion.

That is what I saw on the road.

Not helplessness.

Not surrender.

A country standing at the edge of a new economic chapter, still capable of preserving the American Dream if enough people decide to move before the crowd.

No one is coming to save you.

After meeting the people I met, I no longer see that as bad news.

I see it as the most empowering truth in America.

Your future belongs to you. Work hard, dream. Attain.

www.ingramcontent.com/pod-product-compliance
Lightning Source LLC
LaVergne TN
LVHW050818061126
851857LV00012B/859
9798240935725